Toujours Tingo

By the Same Author

The Meaning of Tingo

Toujours
Tingo

More Extraordinary Words to Change the Way We See the World

Adam Jacot de Boinod

Illustrations: Sandra Howgate

ALLEN LANE
an imprint of
PENGUIN BOOKS

PENGUIN BOOKS

Published by the Penguin Group
Penguin Books Ltd, 80 Strand, London WC2R ORL, England
Penguin Group (USA) Inc., 375 Hudson Street, New York, New York 10014, USA
Penguin Group (Canada), 90 Eglinton Avenue East, Suite 700, Toronto, Ontario,
Canada M4P 2Y3 (a division of Pearson Penguin Canada Inc.)
Penguin Ireland, 25 St Stephen's Green, Dublin 2, Ireland
(a division of Penguin Books Ltd)
Penguin Group (Australia), 250 Camberwell Road, Camberwell,
Victoria 3124, Australia (a division of Pearson Australia Group Pty Ltd)
Penguin Books India Pvt Ltd, 11 Community Centre,
Panchsheel Park, New Delhi – 110 017, India
Penguin Group (NZ), 67 Apollo Drive, Rosedale, North Shore 0632,
New Zealand (a division of Pearson New Zealand Ltd)
Penguin Books (South Africa) (Pty) Ltd, 24 Sturdee Avenue,
Rosebank, Johannesburg 2196, South Africa

Penguin Books Ltd, Registered Offices: 80 Strand, London WC2R ORL, England

www.penguin.com

First published 2007
2

Copyright © Adam Jacot de Boinod, 2007
Illustrations copyright © Sandra Howgate

Set in 8.75/13 pt Swift
Typeset by Andrew Barker
Printed in Great Britain by Clays Ltd, St Ives plc

A CIP catalogue record for this book is available from the British Library

ISBN: 978-0-140-51586-2

In memory of my father

Contents

Foreword

The reception given to my first book, *The Meaning of Tingo*, was very heartening, and encouraged me to continue to explore the wilder hinterlands of the world's more unusual words and expressions. I am glad to say my first foray was by no means exhaustive. Looking further into some of the more common languages I found such delights as **okuri-okami**, the Japanese word for 'a man who feigns thoughtfulness by offering to see a girl home only to try to molest her once he gets in the door' (literally, a see-you-home wolf); **kaelling**, the Danish for 'a woman who stands on the steps of her house yelling obscenities at her kids'; and **belochnik**, the Russian for 'a thief specializing in stealing linen off clothes lines' (an activity that was supposedly very lucrative in the early 1980s).

And how could I have missed the German **Kiebitz**, 'an onlooker at a card game who interferes with unwanted advice' or the Portuguese **pesamenteiro**, 'one who habitually joins groups of mourners at the home of a deceased person, ostensibly to offer condolences but in reality to partake of the refreshments which he expects will be served'?

In this second volume I've ventured too into over a hundred new languages, with African and Native American tongues scoring high with the surprising and delightful definitions. The Ndebele of Southern Africa have the word **dii-koyna**, meaning 'to destroy one's own property in anger', an impulse surely felt by most of us at some time or another, if not acted upon. From the Bakweri language of Cameroon we have **wo-mba**, a charming word to describe 'the smiling in sleep by children'; and from the Buli language of Ghana the verb **pelinti**, 'to move very hot food around inside one's mouth to avoid too close a contact'. And doubtless there are many among us who have found themselves disturbed by a **butika roka** (Gilbertese, Oceania), 'a brother-in-law coming around too often'.

Once again, of course, many of the more unusual words relate closely to the local specifics of their cultures. Most of us are unlikely to need the verb **sendula** (from the Mambwe of Zambia), meaning 'to find accidentally a dead animal in the forest', which carries with it the secondary sense 'and be excited at the thought that a lion or leopard could still be around'; the bizarre noun **mmbwe**, from the Venda of South Africa, which describes 'a round pebble taken from a crocodile's stomach and swallowed by a chief' (which can hardly be an everyday occurrence); or the wonderful and unlikely **biritululo**, from the Kiriwani of Papua New Guinea, meaning 'comparing yams to settle a dispute'. But even if we never have the call to use such expressions, it's surely enriching to know that in Malay **pisan zapra** is 'the time needed to eat a banana'; in Finnish, **poronkusema** is 'the distance equal to how far a reindeer can travel without a comfort break'; while **manàntsona**, from the Malagasy of Madagascar, is 'to smell or sniff before entering a house, as a dog does'.

We may not share the same climate, but we can all too easily imagine the use of words like **hanyauku** (Rukwangali, Namibia), 'to walk on tiptoe on warm sand', **barbaran-on** (Ik, Nilo-Saharan), 'to sit in a group of people warming up in the morning sun', or **dynke** (Norwegian), 'the act of dunking somebody's face in snow'.

Despite our differing circumstances, the words once again reveal that the commonality of human experience remains strong. Most of us know a **poyipoyi** (Tsonga, South Africa), 'a person who talks at length but does not make sense', or a **mutakarrim** (Persian), 'one who makes pretensions to generosity', if not a **kanjus makkhi-chus** (Hindi), 'a person so miserly that if a fly falls into his cup of tea, he'll fish it out and suck it dry before throwing it away'. And we've surely all observed in our friends and colleagues **chovochovo** (Luvale, Zambia), 'the tendency to carry on talking after others have stopped', not to mention **napleiten** (Dutch), 'to discuss might-have-beens, go over old ground again, keep on arguing after a thing has been decided'. And anyone who's ever tried to manage people will have tried **digdig** (Manobo, Philippines), 'to praise someone for the quality he lacks in order to encourage him to develop that quality'.

There must be buses on every route in the world where one can spot a **tyčovka** (Czech), 'a woman who hangs on to the pole next to the bus driver and chats him up'. On Wall Street, American financiers would understand the verb **iwaktehda**, from the Dakotan language of one of their own native peoples, meaning 'to go home in triumph having taken scalps'. And even in the most sophisticated societies there will be plenty who have, at one time or another, experienced the equivalent of the Tsongan **rhwe**, 'to sleep on the floor without a mat and usually drunk and naked'.

Half as long again as *The Meaning of Tingo*, this second bite into the substantial cherry of world languages has allowed me to venture in depth into all sorts of new areas. There are more examples of 'false friends', from the Czech word **host**, which confusingly means 'guest', to the Estonian **sober**, a perhaps unlikely word for 'a male friend'. There are the intriguing meanings of the names of cities and countries, palindromes and even national anthems, as well as a series of worldwide idioms, which join the words in confirming that the challenges, joys and disappointments of human existence are all too similar around the globe. The admonitory 'Don't count your chickens' of English, for example, is echoed in most languages, becoming, in Danish, **man skal ikke sælge skindet, før bjørnen er skudt**, 'one should not sell the fur before the bear has been shot'; in Turkish, **dereyi görmeden paçaları sıvama**, 'don't roll up your trouser legs before you see the stream'; and in the Ndonga language of Namibia, **ino manga ondjupa ongombe inaayi vala**, 'don't hang the churning calabash before the cow has calved'.

At a time when the march of English continues relentlessly through the ever more globalized world, I can only hope to encourage the survival of some of these rare and wonderful languages, which are tragically becoming extinct at the rate of one a fortnight, taking with them such charming and useful concepts as **a' matiti** (Rotuman, South Pacific), 'to accustom a baby to cooler temperatures by taking it on a walk in the early morning', **pikikiwepogosi** (Obijway, North America), 'having the taste of an animal that was tired out before it was killed' and **chaponner** (Gallo, France), 'to stick a finger up a chicken's bottom to see if it is laying an egg'.

English is of course a great language, but we shouldn't be surprised that there are many others too. So let's celebrate the many varieties of women described by the Japanese, from the **kakobijin**, 'the sort of woman who talks incessantly about how she would have been thought of as a stunner if she had lived in a different era, when men's tastes were different' (literally, bygone beauty) to the **nitto-onna**, the 'woman so dedicated to her career that she has no time to iron blouses and so resorts to dressing only in knitted tops'; and relish the precision with which the Germans observe the comings and goings in the relationship circus, from the **Lückenfüller**, 'the person one dates between two serious relationships' (literally, hole-filler) to the **Trennungsagentur**, 'a man hired by women to break the news to their men that they are dumped' (literally, separation agent).

Further afield, we can only sympathize with the poor **gagung**

(Cantonese), 'a man without a woman owing to the inequality of the gender ratio after the One Child policy' (literally, bare branches); try to understand **oka/shete** (Ndonga, Namibia), 'urination difficulties caused by eating frogs before the rain has duly fallen'; cherish the thought of the **echafouréré** (Gallo, France), 'tickled cat hiding under the table or chair'; and be impressed by **gintawan** (Manobo, Philippines), 'the energy and industry of the first wife (when her husband takes an additional wife) as a result of the competition from the second wife'.

I can only hope that if this book doesn't make you **elmosolyodik** (Hungarian), 'break into a smile', or bring on an attack of **latterkrampe** (Norwegian), 'convulsive laughter', it doesn't reduce you to **gegemena** (Rukwangali, Namibia), 'muttering while sobbing' or even make you **jera** (Indonesian), 'so scared by a past experience that one will never want to do it again'.

Adam Jacot de Boinod

As before, I've done my level best to check the accuracy of all the words included, but, if you have any comments, suggestions for changes, or even favourite examples of words of your own, please do get in touch with me at my website (**www.themeaningoftingo. com**). There were some very helpful – and on occasion enlightening – responses to the first book, for which I remain very grateful. Thank you also for some great new words.

Acknowledgements

I am deeply grateful to the following people for their advice and help: Giles Andreae, Suzy Barry, Karen Coster, Caroline Harris, Dr Muge Kinacioglu, Pierre-Yves Kohler, Therese Larsson, Kate Lawson, Sarah McDougall, Zahra Naderi, Karen Naundorf, James Nixey, Vicky Rigby, Mary and Gordon Snow, Sion Williams and Anette Wilms; and as well many of the professors at the School of Oriental and African Studies, London and staff at the BBC World Service.

In particular I must thank my illustrator, Sandra Howgate, my agent, Peter Straus, my excellent editor at Penguin, Georgina Laycock; and once again my collaborator, Mark McCrum, for his fine work on the text.

I.
Getting Acquainted

bie shi rongyi; jian shi nan (*Chinese*)
parting is easy but meeting is difficult

Hamjambo

However good or bad we're feeling inside, we still have to communicate with each other. We come out of our front door, see someone and adopt the public face. 'How are you?' 'Awright, mate?' we ask at home. Abroad, greetings seem somehow more exotic:

stonko?	Muskogee (Oklahoma and Florida, USA)
ah chop?	Aramaic (Maaloula, Syria)
oli?	Koyo (Congo)
hamjambo?	Kiswahili (South East Africa)

'Fine, thanks!' we reply. They say:

bare bra	Norwegian
dagu dad	Adyghe (North Caucasus, Russia)
bash	Kurdi (Iran, Iraq)

How is your nose?

The Onge of the Andaman Islands don't ask 'How are you?' but 'How is your nose?' The correct response is to reply that you are 'heavy with odour'. Around the world there are numerous other ways to meet and greet:

cead mile failte (Irish) one hundred thousand welcomes

añjalikā (Pali, India) the raising of the hands as a sign of greeting

inga i moana (Gilbertese, Oceania) to greet with open arms but soon tire of

er-kas (Pahlavi, Iran) hands under the armpits in respectful salutation

abruzo (Latin American Spanish) the strong hug men give each other whenever they meet

lamuka usalali (Mambwe, Zambia) to greet somebody lying down on one's back (a salute generally given to chiefs)

'And this is ...'

The Scots have a useful word, **tartle**, which means to hesitate in recognizing a person or thing, as happens when you are introducing someone whose name you can't quite remember. They are not the only ones to suffer from this infuriating problem:

ciniweno (Bemba, Zambia) a thing, the name of which one does not remember

joca (Portuguese) thingumajig, thingumabob

Tongue-tied

That little dilemma solved, not everyone finds it easy to continue:

byatabyata (Tsonga, South Africa) to try to say something but fail for lack of words

vóvôhetâhtsenáotse (Cheyenne, USA) to prepare the mouth before speaking (for example, by moving or licking one's lips)

dabodela (Malagasy, Madagascar) one in the habit of opening his mouth so as to show his tongue projecting and rolling a little beyond the teeth, and yet not able to speak

bunhan bunahan (Boro, India) to be about to speak and about not to speak

Chatterbox

With others you sometimes wish they found self-expression harder:

láu táu (Vietnamese) to talk fast and thoughtlessly

hablar hasta por los codos (Spanish) to talk non-stop (literally, to talk even through the elbows)

mae hi'n siarad fel melin bupur (Welsh) she talks non-stop (literally, she talks like a pepper mill)

hinikiza (Swahili) to out-talk a person by making a noise

kumoo musu baa (Mandinka, West Africa) to jump into a conversation without knowing the background

nudnyi (Russian) someone who, when asked how they are, tells you in detail

chovochovo (Luvale, Zambia) the tendency to carry on talking after others have stopped

gnagsår i ørene (Norwegian) blisters in your ears: what someone who talks a lot gives you

What's in a name?

First impressions are important, particularly to the people visiting a place for the first time. The name of the Canary Islands (Islands of the Dogs) derives from the wild dogs (**canes**) that barked savagely at the Romans when they first arrived on Gran Canaria.

Cities

Cuzco (Quechuan, Andes) navel of the earth
Khartoum (Arabic) elephant's trunk
Topeka, Kansas (Sioux Indian) a good place to grow potatoes

Countries

Anguilla: from the Spanish for eel, so named by Columbus
  due to its elongated shape
Cameroon: from the Portuguese **Rio de Camarões**, River of
  Shrimps
Faroe Islands: from the Faroese **Føroyar**, Sheep Islands
Barbados: from the name **Os Barbados**, the Bearded Ones:
  the island's fig trees sported long roots resembling beards

Keeping in touch

Advances in technology have ensured that we are always on call, but whether that improves the quality of our lives is somewhat debatable:

yuppienalle (Swedish) a mobile phone (literally, yuppie teddy: as they were like security blankets for yuppies when they first came out)

proverka sloukha (Russian) an expression used in telephone conversations, meaning 'I have nothing special to say – I just called to say hello' (literally, a hearing test)

telebabad (Tagalog, Philippines) talking on the phone for a long time

prozvonit (Czech and Slovak) to call someone's mobile from your own to leave your number in their phone's memory, without the intention of the other person picking up

Tower of Babble

Not that we should ever take communication of any kind for grant-ed. At whatever pace, misunderstandings are all too easy:

geop (Gaelic) fast talk which is mostly unintelligible

beròhina (Malagasy, Madagascar) to be spoken to in a strange dialect, to be perplexed by hearing provincialisms

betenger (Manobo, Philippines) to speak another language with a pronunciation that reflects one's own native language

tener papas en la boca (Chilean Spanish) to speak in a stuffy or incomprehensible manner (literally, to have potatoes in the mouth)

False friends

Those who learn languages other than their own will some-times come across words which look or sound the same as English, but mean very different things:

dating (Tagalog, Philippines) arrival

phrase (French) sentence

dating (Chinese) to ask about, enquire

Handy (German) mobile phone

Baloney

And sometimes people just speak rubbish anyway:

höpöhöpö (Finnish) nonsense

prietpraat (Dutch) twaddle

botalo (Russian) a chatterbox, a babbler (literally, a cowbell)

poyipoyi (Tsonga, South Africa) a person who talks at length but does not make sense

bablat (Hebrew) baloney (an acronym of **Beelbool Beytseem Le-Io Takhleet**: bothering someone's testicles for no reason)

ich verstehe nur Wortsalat (German) I don't understand a thing you are saying (literally, all I hear is the word salad)

Q and A

Information is power, they tell us; but finding out what we need to know isn't always as straightforward as we'd like. Sometimes we have to adopt special methods:

candrānā (Hindi) to make an enquiry with a feigned air of ignorance

antsafa (Malagasy, Madagascar) enquiries about things of which one is fully cognisant beforehand

… although of course two can play at that game:

gadrii nombor shulen jongu (Tibetan) giving an answer that is unrelated to the question (literally, to give a green answer to a blue question)

kinkens (Scots) an evasive answer to an inquisitive child

iqsuktuq (Iñupiat, Inuit) to respond negatively by wrinkling the nose

Mhm mmm

So sometimes it's 'yes' …

mhm	Lithuanian
hooo	Agua Caliente (California, USA)
ow	Amharic (Ethiopia)
eeyee	Setswana (Botswana)
uh-uh-huh	Tamashek (West Africa)

… and other times 'no':

mmm	Pulawat (Micronesia)
uh uh	Shimasiwa (Comoros, Indian Ocean)
yox	Azerbaijani
bobo	Bété (Cameroon)
doo-yee	Kato (California, USA)
halo	Chinook (North America)
pepe	Chitonga (Zambia)
hindi	Tagalog (Philippines)
yuk	Tatar (Russia)

Just be sure you know which m(h)mm is which.

It's all Greek to me

People fail to understand each other all the time it seems. The English idiom 'it's all Greek to me' has counterparts throughout the languages of Europe. To the Germans it's 'Spanish', to the Spanish and Hungarians it's 'Chinese', to the French it's 'Hebrew', to the Poles it's 'a Turkish sermon'. And, more unusually still, the Germans say

ich verstehe nur Bahnhof I only understand station

2.
The Human Condition

ge ru-wa nhagi mo choe
(*Dzongkha, Bhutan*)
the nose doesn't smell the rotting head

Tightwad

However much we like to think that all those odd-looking, strange-speaking people around the world are different from us, the shocking evidence from language is that we are all too similar. Don't most of us, whether we live in city, shanty-town or rural bliss, know one of these?

hallab el-nammleh (Syrian Arabic) a miserly person (literally, ant milker)

krentenkakker (Dutch) one who doesn't like spending money (literally, someone who shits raisins)

kanjus makkhichus (Hindi) a person so miserly that if a fly falls into his cup of tea, he'll fish it out and suck it dry before throwing it away

yaalik (Buli, Ghana) sponging, always expecting help or gifts from others without being willing to offer help

False friends

ego (Rapanui, Easter Island) slightly soiled
hiya (Tagalog, Philippines) bashful
incoherent (French) inconsistent
liar (Malay) undomesticated
um (Bosnian) mind, intellect
slug (Swedish) astute

Big-hearted

Fortunately, those are not the only kind of people on our beautiful and fragile planet:

pagad (Manobo, Philippines) to show consideration for a slow-walking person by also walking slowly, so that he can keep up

manàra-drìmitra (Malagasy, Madagascar) to involve oneself in another's calamity by seeking to extricate him

elunud (Manobo, Philippines) to go deliberately to someone's aid and share in his misfortune, regardless of the obviously ill-fated outcome

Ulterior motive

If only people displaying such fine qualities were always pure of heart. But the Italians are not the only ones who understand **carita pelosa**, generosity with an ulterior motive:

mutakarrim (Persian) one who makes pretensions to generosity

Tantenverführer (German) a young man of excessively good manners whom you suspect of devious motives (literally, aunt seducer)

uunguta (Yamana, Chile) to give much more to one than to others

Obligation

Then again, sometimes the totally sincere can be altogether too much:

Bärendienst (German) an act someone does for you thinking they are doing you a favour, but which you really didn't want them to do

arigata-meiwaku (Japanese) an act someone does for you thinking they are doing you a favour, but which you really didn't want them to do; added to which, social convention now requires you to express suitable gratitude in return

Watching the English

In Greek **megla** (derived from 'made in England') denotes elegance and supreme quality and **jampa** (derived from 'made in Japan') means very cheap. Other languages use rather different standards of Englishness in their idioms:

s kliden Angličana (Czech) as calm as an Englishman
ubbriaco come un marinaio inglese (Italian) as drunk as an English sailor
filer à l'anglaise (French) to slip away like the English

Hat over the windmill

Rather than being a sucker who takes consideration for other people's feelings too far, perhaps it would be better to be one of those enviable individuals who simply doesn't give a damn?

menefreghista (Italian) a person who has an 'I don't care' attitude

piitaamaton (Finnish) unconcerned about other people's feelings

i v oos nye doot (Russian) not to give a damn (literally, it doesn't blow in one's moustache)

no me importa un pepino (Spanish) I don't care two hoots (literally, I don't care a cucumber)

jeter son bonnet par-dessus les moulins (French) to throw caution to the winds (literally, to throw one's hat over the windmills)

Number one

On second thoughts, perhaps not. For the line between self-confidence and self-centredness is always horribly thin:

szakbarbár (Hungarian) a crank who can think of nothing but his/her subject

iakićaghećha (Dakota, USA) one who is unreasonable in his demands, one who keeps asking for things after he should stop

kverulant (Czech) a chronic complainer, a litigious person

hesomagari (Japanese) perverse or cantankerous (literally, bent belly button)

Warm showerer

The Germans have pinpointed some particularly egotistic types:

Klugscheisser someone who always knows best (literally, smart shitter)

Warmduscher someone who is easy on himself (literally, warm showerer)

Trittbrettfahrer to take advantage of someone else's efforts without contributing anything (literally, the person who rides on the stepping board of a bus or train without buying a ticket)

Nose in the clouds

And it's another short step from egotism to conceit:

péter plus haut que son cul (French) to think highly of
yourself (literally, to fart higher than your arse)

creerse la ultima Coca-Cola en el desierto (Central
American Spanish) to have a very high opinion of oneself
(literally, to think one is the last Coca-Cola in the desert)

nosom para oblake (Serbian) he's conceited, puffed up (literally, he's ripping clouds with his nose)

khenh khang (Vietnamese) to walk slowly like an important
person, to put on airs

cuello duro (Spanish) a snob, stuck-up (literally, hard or stiff
neck – from keeping one's nose in the air)

Impressing

Almost as irritating as the conceited and the pompous are those
who fail to see that, as they say in the Kannada language of Southern
India, '**Tumbida koDa tuLukuvudilla**', the pot which is full does
not splash:

farolero (Spanish) a show-off (literally, a lantern maker)

m'as-tu-vu (French) a show-off (literally, one who constantly
asks other people 'Did you see me?')

Spesenritter (German) someone who shows off by paying the
bill on the firm's money (literally, expense knight)

poshlost (Russian) ostentatious bad taste

jor-joran (Indonesian) to compete in showing off one's wealth

elintasokilpailu (Finnish) keeping up with the Joneses

Sucking up

And yet, despite their obvious failings, both snobs and show-offs are often surrounded by the human equivalent of a benign parasite. As the Spanish say, '**La lisonja hace amigos, y la verdad enemigos**', flattery makes friends and truth makes enemies:

chupamedias (Chilean Spanish) a sycophant (literally, sock sucker)
banhista (Portuguese) someone who soft-soaps another
digdig (Manobo, Philippines) to praise a person for the quality which he lacks in order to encourage him to develop that quality
jijirika (Chichewa, Malawi) to curry favour by doing more than expected, but not necessarily well

Eejit

Can it get worse? Unfortunately it can:

lū-lū (Hindi) an idiot, nincompoop
gugbe janjou (Tibetan) a stupid person trying to be clever
kaptsn (Yiddish) one who does not amount to anything and never will
eldhus-fifi (Old Icelandic) an idiot who sits all day by the fire
el semaforo de medianoche (Venezuelan Spanish) a person no one respects and of whom everyone takes advantage, a pushover (literally, traffic light at midnight)

Salt in the pumpkin

'It is foolish to deal with a fool,' say the practical Japanese, though the Chinese wisely observe that 'He who asks is a fool for five minutes, but he who does not ask remains a fool forever.' Such observations reveal what the Catalans call **seny**, a canny common sense. Others value such qualities too:

ha sale in zucca (Italian) he has common sense (literally, he's got salt in the pumpkin)
lapchaty goos (Russian) a sly old fox (literally, a cunning goose)
baser (Arabic) one with great insight or one who is blind

Idiot savant

In Italy you are **stupido come l'acqua dei maccheroni**, as stupid as macaroni water; in Lithuania, **kvailas kaip žąsis**, as silly as a goose; while in France you can be as stupid as **une cruche** (a pitcher), **un pot** (a pot) or **un chou** (a cabbage). But even idiots are not necessarily all they seem:

adalahendry (Malagasy, Madagascar) a person ignorant yet wise in some things
Spruchkasper (German) a fool full of wise sayings
apo trelo kai apo pedi mathenis tin aletheia (Greek proverb) from a crazy person and from children you learn the truth

Pregnant birds

Although the very young can delight us with their wonderful and surprising remarks, naivety is not, sadly, a state of mind that will work for a lifetime:

creer en pajaritos preñados (Venezuelan Spanish) to be credulous (literally, to believe in pregnant birds)

yelang zida (Chinese) ludicrous conceit stemming from pure ignorance

lolo (Hawaiian Pidgin) someone who would be glad to give you the time of day, if he knew how to read a clock

A piece of bread

How wonderful it is when we meet that rare person who just gets it right all the time:

katundu (Chichewa, Malawi) a person with outstanding positive qualities

Lieblingsstück (German) the favourite item of a collection (said of someone special)

para quitar el hipo (Latin American Spanish) very impressive; astonishing (literally, enough to cure the hiccups)

es un pedazo de pan (Spanish) he/she's a good person/it's a good thing (literally, he/she/it is a piece of bread)

A leopard cannot change its spots

chassez le naturel, il revient au gallop (French) chase away the natural and it returns at a gallop

aus einem Ackergaul kann man kein Rennpferd machen (Swabian German) you cannot turn a farm horse into a racehorse

dhanab al kalb a 'waj walaw hattaytu fi khamsin galib (Arabic) the dog's tail remains crooked even if it's put in fifty moulds

vuk dlaku mijenja ali æud nikada (Croatian) a wolf changes his coat but not his attitude

die Katze lässt das Mausen nicht (German) the cat will not abandon its habit of chasing mice

chi nasce quadrato non muore tondo (Italian) if you are born square you don't die round

karishkirdi kancha baksang dele tokoigo kachat (Kyrgyz) no matter how well you feed a wolf it always looks at the forest

gorbatogo mogila ispravit (Russian) only the grave will cure the hunchback

3.
Emotional Intelligence

wie boter op zijn hoofd heeft,
moet niet in de zon lopen (*Dutch*)
those who have butter on their head should
not run around under the sun

Happy valley

Whatever kind of character we've been blessed with, we all still experience similar highs and lows of emotion. Pure happiness is a wonderful thing; and we should never take it for granted, for who knows how long it may last?

kusamba (Ngangela, Angola) to skip, gambol, express uninhibited joy

sungumuka (Luvale, Zambia) to experience transitory pleasure in the novel

faly ambonindoza (Malagasy, Madagascar) delight before the danger is passed, premature joy

choi lu bù (Vietnamese) to have round after round of fun

alegria secreta candela muerta (Spanish proverb) unshared joy is an unlighted candle

In the coal cellar

The opposite emotion is rarely sought, but it arrives all the same:

at være i kulkælderen (Danish) to be very sad or depressed
(literally, to be in the coal cellar)

lalew (Manobo, Philippines) to grieve over something to the
extent that one doesn't eat

dastehen wie ein begossener Pudel (German) to look
depressed (literally, to stand there like a soaked poodle)

mal ikke fanden på veggen (Norwegian) to be very pessi-
mistic (literally, to paint the devil on the wall)

dar lástima (Latin American Spanish) to be in such a bad way
that people feel sorry for you

False friends

bang (Dutch) afraid

blag (Haitian Creole) joke

puke (Rotuman, South Pacific) to come strongly over one (of
feelings)

drift (Dutch) passion

job (Mongolian) correct, good

meal (Gaelic) to enjoy

Boo-hoo

Sometimes the best course is just to let it all hang out:

kutar-atugutata (Yamana, Chile) to get hoarse from much crying

gegemena (Rukwangali, Namibia) to mutter while sobbing

sekgamatha (Setswana, Botswana) the dirtiness of the face and eyes from much crying

dusi (Malay) to be perpetually crying (of young children)

āpaddharm (Hindi) a conduct permissible only in times of extreme distress

Crocodile

Though even tears are never as straightforward as we might like them to be:

ilonkyynelet (Finnish) tears of joy

miangòtingòtim-bòninàhitra (Malagasy, Madagascar) to weep in order to get something

chantepleurer (French) to sing and weep simultaneously

Smiley

'Cheer up!' we tell each other. And hopefully this brings the right results:

elmosolyodik (Hungarian) to break into a smile
sogo o kuzusu (Japanese) to smile with delight (literally, to demolish one's face)
cuòi khì (Vietnamese) to laugh a silly laugh

German Blues

The idioms of the world are full of colour. But in Germany 'blue' has a rich range of uses:

blaue vom Himmel herunter lügen to lie constantly (literally, to lie the blue out of the sky)
grün und blau ärgern sich to see red (literally, to anger oneself green and blue)
blau machen to take a day off (literally, to make blue)
blau sein to be drunk (literally, to be blue)
mit einem blauen Auge davon kommen to get off unscathed (literally, to get away with a blue eye)
ein blaues Auge a black eye (literally, a blue eye)
die blaue Stunde the time before dusk especially during winter (literally, the blue hour)

Tee-hee

Sometimes, indeed, more than the right results:

bungisngís (Tagalog, Philippines) one who giggles at the slightest provocation

ngisngis (Manobo, Philippines) someone who cannot control his laughter

latterkrampe (Norwegian) convulsive laughter

mengare (Gilbertese, Oceania) a forced laugh, to laugh on the wrong side of one's mouth

tirebouchonnant (French) extremely funny (literally, like a corkscrew – as one takes in air repeatedly to laugh)

mémêstátamaò'o (Cheyenne, USA) to laugh so hard that you fart

No potato

In the Arab world they distinguish between those who are good-humoured, **damak khafeef**, literally, their blood is light, and the opposite, **damak tieel**, their blood is heavy. But however well-meaning, humour always carries the risk of failure:

pikun (Kapampangan, Philippines) one who cannot take a joke

nye kartoshka (Russian) no joking matter (literally, no potato)

jayus (Indonesian) someone who tries to make a joke which is so unfunny that you laugh anyway

Pulling your nose

The different expressions for 'pulling someone's leg' reveal subtle differences in approaches to teasing. For the Germans it's **jemandem einen Bären aufbinden**, literally, to sell somebody a bear; for the French it's **mettre en boite**, to put someone in a box. The Spanish pull your hair (**tomar el pelo**), the Finns pull your nose (**vetää nenästä**), while the Czechs go one further and hang balls on your nose (**věšet bulíky na nos**).

Worry-wart

But better, surely, to laugh at your troubles than live on your nerves:

bēi gōng shé yǐng (Chinese) worrying about things that aren't there (literally, seeing the reflection of a bow in a cup and thinking it's a snake)

qaquablaabnaqtuq (Iñupiat, Inuit) to be tense because of an impending unpleasantness

doki doki (Japanese) the feeling of great anxiety when someone is about to do or doing something very nerve-racking

hira hira (Japanese) the feeling you get when you walk into a dark and decrepit old house in the middle of the night

como cocodrilo en fabrica de carteras (Puerto Rican Spanish) to be extremely nervous (literally, to be like a crocodile in a wallet factory)

No balls

We all aspire to **zanshin** (Japanese), a state of relaxed mental alertness in the face of danger; but for most of us our reactions are all too human when bad things really do happen:

les avoir à zéro (French) to be frightened (literally, to have one's testicles down to zero)

ngua mat (Vietnamese) unable to stand something shocking

khankhanana (Tsonga, South Africa) to fall backwards rigid (as in a fit or from extreme fright)

jera (Indonesian) so scared by a past experience that one will never want to do it again

Spider on the ceiling

Then again, rather be healthily scared than driven round the bend:

keçileri kaçırma (Turkish) to lose one's marbles (literally, to kidnap the goats)

avoir une araignée au plafond (French) to be crazy (literally, to have a spider on the ceiling)

lud ko struja (Serbian) crazy as electricity

más loco que un plumero (Spanish) crazier than a feather duster

vrane su mu popile mozak (Croatian) he's crazy (literally, cows have drunk his brain)

A sandwich short of a picnic

šplouchá mu na maják (Czech) it's splashing on his lighthouse

hij heeft een klap van de molen gehad (Dutch) he got a blow from the windmill

ne pas avoir inventé le fil à couper le beurre (French) not to have invented the cheese wire to cut butter

hu khay beseret (Hebrew) he lives in a movie; his whole life is like a movie

non avere tutti i venerdì (Italian) to be lacking some Fridays

tem macaquinhos no sotão (Portuguese) he has little monkeys in the attic

udaren mokrom čarapom (Serbian) hit with a wet sock

ikke at være den skarpeste kniv i skuffen (Danish) not to be the sharpest knife in the drawer

4.
Social Animals

ui mai koe ki ahau he aha te mea nui
o te ao, māku e kī atu he tangata, he
tangata, he tangata! (*Maori*)
ask me what is the greatest thing in the world,
I will reply: it is people, it is people, it is people!

Most of us are sociable creatures, unable to avoid relying on those around us to keep us happy:

bukaladza (Tsonga, South Africa) to dispel boredom by doing something such as paying a visit

buren (Dutch) to look in upon one's neighbours

lishashamana (Lozi, Niger-Congo) the habit of running out to see anything that happens

gezellig (Dutch) an atmosphere of cosiness, of being with good friends, and spending time together laughing and having fun; the kind of moments that create memories

Hermit

Better that than being the odd one out:

lappsjuka (Swedish) a state of melancholy through being so isolated

encontrarse como un pulpo en un garaje (Spanish) to be like a fish out of water (literally, to be like an octopus in a garage)

nkunkula pansi (Mambwe, Zambia) an orphan who has no one to look after him and passes his time playing in the dust

Whacking aunt

When we do get together, are our conversations as morally improving as they might be?

gigirhi-gigirhi (Tsonga, South Africa) to go from village to village exchanging gossip

Klatschbase (German) a person who always gossips (literally, whacking aunt)

ngasngás (Tagalog, Philippines) a scandal caused by gossip

Bären aufbinden (German) to tell false tales (literally, to tie a bear onto someone)

False friends

sober (Estonian) male friend
drug (Russian) good friend
fun (Yoruba, Nigeria, Benin and Togo) to give
host (Czech) guest

Party spirit

For some the urge to socialize can get the better of their wiser instincts:

mawadishiweshkiwin (Ojibway, North America) the habit of making visits too often

mit der Tür ins Haus (German) failing to take someone by surprise, to be too direct, to be too forward (literally, to fall with the door into the house)

paglaguma (Tagalog, Philippines) the act of joining others in a party although uninvited

paracaidista (Central American Spanish) a freeloader, gate-crasher; also someone who jumps into a discussion without knowing anything about the subject (literally, parachutist)

Storm-free shack

But then who can resist a really good bash?

parapetowka (Polish) the first party in someone's new apartment (literally, a windowsiller – as there's no furniture yet)

ipeje (Yoruba, Nigeria, Benin and Togo) an invitation to a banquet

ponkal (Tamil) a boiling, a bubbling-up; a great festival in honour of the sun entering the sign Capricorn (the name comes from the cooking of the celebratory rice)

eine sturmfreie Bude (German) a flat without the parents, thus allowing the children to throw a party (literally, a storm-free shack)

nachspil (Swedish) a follow-up party

After-parties

In Japan, the second, sometimes spontaneous gathering that happens after you have left the main party is called **nijikai**. If you move on after a while to a third place, it's called **sanjikai**.

Looking over the fence

Some guests are obviously more welcome than others:

partigangare (Swedish) a fanatical partygoer
laumaeläin (Finnish) a gregarious animal
Zaungast (German) a guest who looks over the fence to get at least the music of the party (literally, fence guest)
aguafiestas (Spanish) a killjoy, one who throws water on a party (literally, water party)

The sound of yoghurt

A little music often helps …

kanariom (Yoeme, USA and Mexico) the first tune played or danced
dorremifassolar (Portuguese) to play scales on the piano
yaourt (French) English pop music sung without any understanding of the meaning; singing to create something that sounds like English pop music but actually isn't (literally, yoghurt)
accharika (Pali, India) to make heavenly music

Wiggle your bucket

... and then things can really kick off:

gida (South Africa Township) to jump up and down constantly
in one place (as a form of dance)

menear el bote (Mexican Spanish) to dance (literally, to
wiggle your bucket)

chachula (Tsonga, South Africa) a dance with the rhythmic
quivering of the body

kundáy (Tagalog, Philippines) dance movements made by the
wrist

Duck feet

Or not, as the case may be:

hávêsévôhomo'he (Cheyenne, USA) to dance badly

asiqtuq (Iñupiat, Inuit) nodding with the head while others dance

pamutas-silya (Tagalog, Philippines) ladies who go to dances but do not dance

paton (Cuban Spanish) duck feet (i.e. can't dance)

Keeping their bottle

Sometimes you just have to call in the professionals:

binasohan (Bikol, Philippines) a dance in which three glasses partially filled with wine are balanced, one on the head and one on each hand

danza de la botella (Paraguayan Spanish) a bottle dance in which each dancer balances a flower-filled bottle on his head

gamadj (Ojibway, North America) dancing with a scalp in one's hands, in order to receive some presents

National anthems

The title of a country's officially chosen anthem can be very revealing about its history: the Czech **Kde domov můj** (Where is My Home) reflects many years of shifting borders and invasions. Other interesting titles include:

Burkina Faso: **Une seule nuit** (Just One Night)
Israel: **Hatikvah** (The Hope)
Kurdistan: **Ey Reqîb** (Hey Enemy or Hey Guardian)
Netherlands: **Het Wilhemus** (The William)
Norway: **Ja, vi elsker dette landet** (Yes, We Love This
    Country)
Romania: **Deşteaptă-te, Române** (Wake Up, Romanian)
Tuva, Siberia: **Tooruktug Dolgay Tangdym** (The Forest is
    Full of Pine Nuts)

Time, please

Always be wary of overstaying your welcome. As the Italians say, **'L'ospite è come il pesce: dopo tre giorni puzza'**, the guest is like a fish: after three days he smells bad:

desconvidar (Portuguese) to withdraw an invitation

il est comme un cheveu dans la soupe (French) he is not welcome; he has come at an awkward time (literally, he is like a hair in the soup)

pudyapudya (Tsonga, South Africa) to go away because one is shown one is not wanted

ngloyor (Indonesian) to go without saying goodbye

apagavelas (Caribbean Spanish) the last person to leave a party

Have your cake and eat it

auf zwei Hochzeiten tanzen (German) to dance at two
   weddings

aam ke aam, guthliyon ke daam (Hindi) you can have
   mangoes and sell the seeds as well

dikasih hati minta jantung (Indonesian) given the liver
   and demands the heart

avoir le beurre, argent du beurre et la crémière avec
   (French) to have butter, money from butter, and the woman
   who makes the butter

non si puo avere la botte piena è la moglie ubriaca
   (Italian) you can't have a full cask of wine and a drunken
   wife

5.
Having an
Argument

casa onde não há pão, todos ralham
e ninguém tem razão (*Portuguese*)
*in a breadless home, everyone complains and
nobody is right*

Cold porridge

One downside to socializing is all the enforced jollity, often with people you might not choose to spend that much time with otherwise:

metepatas (Spanish) a person who always does or says the wrong thing

yokogamiyaburi (Japanese) an obstinate person (literally, to be difficult to tear paper sideways)

elle coupe les cheveux en quatre (French) she is a difficult person (literally, she cuts hair into four pieces)

kashi nye svarit (Russian) to be impossible to get along with (literally, the porridge can't be boiled)

Being difficult

The German expression **Fisimatenten machen**, meaning to make things unnecessarily difficult, is a mangling of the French **visiter ma tante** (visit my aunt). It originates in the difficulty of imposing a curfew on occupied France during the Second World War. **Visiter ma tante** was the general excuse used by people arrested on the streets at night by French soldiers.

On the edge

Watch out for those snappy exclamations. They're generally a sign of rapidly fading patience:

kalter Kaffe (German) that's old hat (literally, cold coffee)
dang-geun i-ji (Korean) it's obvious (literally, it's a carrot)

da lichen die Hühner (German) you must be joking
(literally, this makes the chickens laugh)
heso de cha o wakasu (Japanese) don't make me laugh
(literally, I boil tea in my navel)
nu tog fan bofinken (Swedish) now that's done it (literally,
the devil took the chaffinch)
ne cui hui v chai (Russian) don't mess things up (literally,
don't stir the tea with your penis)

Looking for the hair

And some people just can't help but provoke you:

bamp (Scots) to harp on the same topic constantly, to nag about the same thing

chercher un poil aux oeufs (French) to nit-pick (literally, to look for a hair on eggs)

juubakonosumi o (yoojide) tsutsuku (Japanese) to split hairs (literally, to pick at the corners of a food-serving box with a toothpick)

no tener pelos en la lengua (Latin American Spanish) to be very outspoken (literally, to have no hairs on your tongue)

napleiten (Dutch) to discuss might-have-beens, go over old ground again, keep on arguing after a thing has been decided

Pig's ribbon

Sometimes you can feel it all getting too much:

la moutarde me monte au nez (French) to begin to lose one's temper (literally, mustard is climbing up my nose)

akaspa (Dakota, USA) to be provoked beyond endurance

poner como lazo de cochino a (alguien) (Mexican Spanish) to jump down someone's throat (literally, to make someone look like a pig's ribbon)

Cracking up

We must, of course, do our very best to be tactful and discreet, relying on our wits to keep us out of trouble:

mijèry àrina an-tàva (Malagasy, Madagascar) not to tell a person his faults (literally, to notice a blotch on the face but not mention it)

dar(le) el avión a (alguien) (Mexican Spanish) to say yes or agree, without really meaning it or paying attention (literally, to give the aeroplane)

tumodisa (Setswana, Botswana) to shut a person's mouth to prevent him from speaking

ad-hoc-Bildungen (German) making up a new word on the spot in a moment of need

adin' andriana (Malagasy, Madagascar) a quarrel in which both parties show great respect for each other

Hell is other people(s)

It's always easier to describe unpleasant things or experiences in foreign terms; it makes them less immediate and it's a good way of having a dig at another culture at the same time. When we can't understand someone's English we call it Double Dutch; while the Danes call a grey cloudy day Swedish Sunshine:

spaans benauwd (Dutch) lack of air when you are dead nervous (literally, Spanish lack of air)

une querelle d'Allemand (French) a quarrel started for no obvious or good reason (literally, a German argument)

kitaiskyi televizor (Russian) the manual examination of baggage at customs (literally, Chinese television)

mandras kaip prancūzų šuo (Lithuanian) proud as a French dog

avoir l'oeil americain (French) to have a sharp eye (literally, an American eye)

doccia scozzese (Italian) a shower that goes from very hot to very cold (literally, Scottish shower)

schwedische Gardinen (German) prison bars (literally, Swedish curtains – the Swedish had a reputation for fine quality steel)

Mexican rage

Mexican Spanish has expressions for each stage of losing your patience with someone. **Alucinar a alguien** is to be fed up with someone's constant and not very welcome presence; **estar como agua para (pa') chocolate**, to be absolutely furious (literally, to be as hot as the water needed to melt chocolate); and finally **parar(se) de pestañas** describes losing it completely (literally, to stand on your eyelashes).

Picking a fight

The typically polite Japanese use few insults and those they do use tend to be indirect. **Baka** (fool) is a combination of the words for 'horse' and 'deer', with the implication that anyone who cannot tell a horse from a deer is obviously a fool.

Get lost !

Other cultures get straight to the point:

vai à fava (Portuguese) go to the fava bean!
sukse kuuseen (Finnish) ski into a spruce!
ej bekot (Latvian) go mushrooming!
skatertyu droga (Russian) table cloth to the road!

… especially in the Spanish-speaking world:

banarse take a bath!
buscar berros find watercress!
freir bunuelos fry doughnuts!
freir esparragos fry asparagus!
hacer gargaras gargle!
a la goma as far as rubber stretches!

Dumb as bread

The rest of the world is not short of colourful verbal insults. 'May the fleas of a thousand camels infest your armpits,' they say in Arabic; and many other languages compare people to animals when being rude. In French your object of scorn is a **chameau** (camel) or **vache** (cow); in Swahili, a **punda** (zebra); while in Vietnam you call the offender **do cho de**, literally, you dog birth. Other expressions of abuse have clearly exercised the full imagination of the truly upset:

du bist doch dumm wie Brot (German) you are as dumb as bread

korinttiaivot (Finnish) an insult to describe the old (literally, currant brains)

du kannst mir mal in die Schuhe blasen (Swiss German) kiss my arse (literally, you can blow into my shoes)

du kannst mir gern den Buckel runterrutschen und mit der Zunge bremsen (Austrian German) you can slide down my hunchback using your tongue as a brake

Anger-hair

Now things are in danger of getting seriously out of control:

tener una cara de telefono ocupado (Puerto Rican
Spanish) to be angry (literally, to have a face like a busy
telephone)

Gesicht wie ein Feuermelder (German) to be so angry that
one's face turns red (literally, a face like a fire extinguisher)

mencak-mencak (Indonesian) to stamp one's feet on the
ground repeatedly, getting very angry

dohatsu-ten o tsuku (Japanese) to be beside oneself with
rage (literally, anger-hair points to heaven)

mouton enragé (French) maddened sheep (said of an angry
person who is usually calm)

waśihdaka (Dakota, USA) one who gets angry at everything

False friends

twist (Dutch) quarrel, dispute, altercation, wrangle
batman (Turkish) thrust
unfair (Dutch) to hit below the belt
pee (Dutch) to be annoyed
hot (Swedish) threat

The blame game

When the blood is boiling things can get increasingly complicated:

togogata (Yamana, Chile) to turn one's attention and anger from one person to another

fijoo (Mandinka, West Africa) anger at someone other than the one who caused the anger

babit (Malay) to implicate third parties in a dispute

hewula (Tsonga, South Africa) to shout down one who keeps on arguing after the evidence has shown him to be guilty

Macho moment

Pray God, it doesn't turn physical:

imbang (Malay) reluctant but prepared to fight

makgatlha (Setswana, Botswana) challengers who show their wish to fight by throwing down a handful of earth

dii-konya (Ndebele, Southern Africa) to destroy your own property in anger

lusud (Manobo, Philippines) to go into someone's house to fight them

parandhu parandhu adikkaradhu (Tamil) to fight by jumping and flying in the air

langola (Mambwe, Zambia) to repeatedly throw a man very hard to the ground

sugun (Malay) seizing the hair or throat to force down your adversary

cisanan (Yamana, Chile) a canoe with an avenger of blood in it coming to exact vengeance

The female is the deadlier ...

The Finnish have a wonderful word, **knapsu**, for anything that's not male behaviour. Other cultures are quick to notice the gender-specific:

Stutenbeißen (German) the special behaviour of women in a
rivalry situation (literally, mare biting)

dzinana (Tsonga, South Africa) to pummel one another with
the side of the fists, away from the thumb, as fighting
women do)

vongola (Tsonga, South Africa) to expose the buttocks (which
is done by women as the ultimate insult when they run out
of invective)

agarrar(se) del chongo (Latin American Spanish) to brawl,
to fight – applied to women (literally, to grab each other by
the bun of the hair

The flapping of wings

Whatever sex we are, we sometimes can't resist having the last word:

kulumbana (Tsonga, South Africa) to follow a person who left a meeting in disgust and shout insults and reproaches after him

dar patadas de ahogado (Latin American Spanish) to fight a losing battle (literally, to thrash around uselessly when you'll drown anyway)

aleteo (Caribbean Spanish) the last words in a lost argument (literally, flapping of wings)

The pot calling the kettle black

c'est l'hôpital qui se moque de la Charité (French) it's the
  hospital that mocks Charity

bagoly mondja a verébnek, hogy nagyfejű (Hungarian)
  the owl calls the sparrow big-headed

rugala se sova sjenici (Croatian) the owl mocked the tit

il bue che dice cornuto all'asino (Italian) the ox saying
  'horned' to the donkey

rîde ciob de oală spartă (Romanian) the splinter laughs at
  the broken pot

al jamal ma yishuf sanamu (Arabic) the camel cannot see
  its own hump

ein Esel schimpft den anderen Langohr (German) a donkey gets cross with a rabbit

6.
The Rules of Attraction

a tola e à lettu alcunu rispettu
(*Corsican*)
have no respect at the table and in bed

The Russian word for falling in love, **oupast'**, also means to be at a loss, to understand nothing. Other languages stress the magic of the early stages of the romantic encounter:

koi no yokan (Japanese) a sense on first meeting that something is going to evolve into love

ong buóm (Vietnamese) bees and butterflies, flirtations, love-making

anhimmeln (German) to look enraptured at someone (literally, as if they were the sky)

No-pan kissa

On summer evenings, in little towns in Italy, young men and women **fare la passeggiata**, perambulating the central square sizing each other up and flirting, or, as they say in that country, **fare il galletto**, to do like the rooster. Other societies offer other options:

blyazh (Russian) a beach where girls can be picked up

kamáki (Greek) the young local guys strolling up and down beaches hunting for female tourists (literally, harpoons)

no-pan kissa (Japanese) coffee shops with mirrored floors to allow customers to look up waitresses' skirts

tyčovka (Czech) a woman who hangs on to the pole next to the bus driver and chats him up

Like a motorway

In Indonesia, they have a word for falling in love at first sight: **kepincut**. But when it comes to what's most attractive in a woman, there seems to be no accounting for tastes:

rombhoru (Bengali) a woman having thighs as well-shaped as banana trees

autostrada (Italian) a very slender girl without pronounced sexual attributes (literally, a motorway)

e thamba (Oshindonga, Namibia) a big, fat and clean girl

baffona (Italian) an attractive moustachioed woman

at have både til gården og til gaden (Danish) a woman well equipped both at the front and the rear (literally, to have both to the courtyard and to the street)

Double take

Certainly, caution is advised in the early stages:

layogenic (Tagalog, Philippines) someone good-looking from afar but not up close

daburu bikkuri (Japanese) women who, as they are approaching a stall, look so attractive that they give the vendor a shock, but when they finally arrive at his counter they give him another shock as the scales fall from his eyes (literally, double shock)

A face only a mother could love

And one should always be wary of a blind date:

kakobijin (Japanese) the sort of woman who talks incessantly about how she would have been thought of as a stunner if she had lived in a different era, when men's tastes in women were different (literally, bygone beauty)

kimangamanga (Gilbertese, Oceania) a person with a ridiculous walk and defective bottom

sjøstygg (Norwegian) being so ugly that the tide won't come in if you're on the shore (literally, sea ugly)

skreeulelik (Afrikaans) scream ugly (i.e. so frightening as to make the viewer scream)

être moche à caler des roués de corbillard (French) to be extremely ugly (literally, to be ugly enough to stop the wheels of a hearse)

Diving fish, swooping geese

In China, many hundreds of years ago, a poet said of the great beauty Hsi Chi that when she went for a walk fish dived deeper, geese swooped off their course, and deer ran into the forest before her beauty. Therefore, instead of saying a woman is as beautiful as Hsi Chi, in Chinese one simply says the four words **ch'en yü, le yen**, diving fish, swooping geese.

You beautiful creature

In other languages the comparison with animals may be even more direct. In Arabic, a beautiful woman is spoken of as having **yoon al ghrazaali**, the eyes of the gazelle. Similar metaphorical expressions abound:

miyulesa (Sinhala, Sri Lanka) a woman with eyes like a deer's
omïrïghlïgh (Khakas, Siberia) a person having a beautiful bearing in the same way that a horse has a strong chest
kati-kehari (Hindi) having the waist of an elegant lion (used of an attractive woman)

And what do women want?

The men of the Wodaabe (a nomadic tribe of Central and East Africa) perform the **yaake**, a competition of charm and personality judged by young women. Performing the yaake, a man who can hold one eye still and roll the other is considered particularly alluring by the judges.

karlakarl (Swedish) a real man
bellone (Italian) a hunk who's rather too pleased with himself
tarzan (Hebrew) a dandy
armoire à glace (French) a great hulking brute (literally, a wardrobe of ice cream)

Double Valentine

In Japan, Valentine's Day is celebrated on two different dates: 14 February, when girls are allowed to express their love to boys by presenting chocolate; and 14 March, known as White Day, when the male has to return the gift he received. Chocolates given sincerely on these days are **honmei-choko**, true-feeling chocolates. However, women are also obliged to give chocolates to all the men in their lives, meaning large numbers of co-workers, bosses, etc. These are known as **giri-choko**, obligatory chocolates.

My Japanese stamps

The Hindi language has **sandesh-kāvya**, describing a poetic form where the lover sends his message of love and yearning to his beloved through clouds or birds. The Mailu language of Papua New Guinea has **oriori**, a boy's song to attract a girl. Aspiring Western Romeos often prefer a more basic approach:

war dein Vater ein Dieb? Weil er die Sterne vom Himmel gestohlen hat um sie dir in die Augen zu setzen (German) Was your father a thief? Because he stole the stars from the sky and put them in your eyes

scusa, baci gli sconosciuti? No? Allora, mi presento … (Italian) Excuse me, do you kiss strangers? No? Well, let me introduce myself …

venez voir mes estampes japonaises (French) Why don't you come up and see my Japanese stamps

Hit by a basket

Not all approaches are necessarily welcome:

echar(le) los perros a alguien (Latin American Spanish) to
flirt with, make a pass at someone (literally, to set the dogs
on someone)

oshi no itte (Japanese) to pursue someone aggressively; to
not take no for an answer (literally, pushing and pushing
alone)

dostat košem (Czech) to flirt with or hit on somebody who
isn't interested and turns you down (literally, to be hit by a
basket)

dikupu (Setswana, Botswana) stubs or stumps of hands or
legs (said teasingly by women to a man who shows no interest in them)

Octopussy

And there are some guys who just don't get the message at all:

atracador (Latin American Spanish) a person who feels up a
woman; someone whose sexual advances are heavy-handed
and unwelcome (literally, mugger)

ozhappu edukkaradhu (Tamil) an act of sexual harassment
perpetrated against female passengers in a crowded bus or
train

el pulpo (Spanish) someone who is 'all hands', who likes to
touch women inappropriately (literally, octopus)

Gooseberry

However well or badly it's going, in matters of romance, two's company, but three is very definitely a crowd:

tocar el violin (Chilean Spanish) a person who uncomfortably accompanies an amorous couple (literally, to play the violin)

segurando a vela (Portuguese) to be the third wheel on a date (literally, holding the candle)

False friends

sleep (Afrikaans) girlfriend or boyfriend

tití (Tagalog, Philippines) penis

poluzzione (Italian) semen

Puff (German) brothel

spunk (Scots) a spark of fire

bite (French) penis

chain (Yiddish) charm

See-you-home wolf

Beware those for whom the habit has become more important than the object:

Schuerzenjaeger (German) someone who chases after women (literally, a hunter of aprons)

amoureux d'une chèvre coiffée (French) a man who is attracted to every woman he sees (literally, a lover of a goat whose fur is combed)

buaya darat (Indonesian) a man who fools women into thinking he's a very faithful lover when in fact he goes out with many different women at the same time (literally, land crocodile)

okuri-okami (Japanese) a man who feigns thoughtfulness by offering to see a girl home only to try to molest her once he gets in the door (literally, a see-you-home wolf)

tlazolmiquiztli (Aztec) the stench which emanates from adulterers

No sweat

For the less sophisticated, courtship can be full of confusing obstacles and hard work:

castigar (Latin American Spanish) purposely to ignore your boyfriend or girlfriend in order to heighten their yearning for you

janeleiro (Portuguese) said of one who spends a lot of time at the front window, especially a young woman who is something of a coquette

talisuyò (Tagalog, Philippines) the work done by a man to win a lady's hand

shvitzer (Yiddish) someone who sweats a lot (especially a nervous seducer)

otenkiya (Japanese) someone who blows hot and cold (literally, weatherman)

Peppery-hot

So we can only hope that sincere feeling will win the day:

cay (Vietnamese) to be peppery-hot; to have a passion for

an jemandem einen Affen gefressen haben (German) to be infatuated with someone (literally, to have eaten a monkey in someone)

ciğerimin köşesinden (Turkish) to love someone from the bottom of your heart (literally, from the corner of your liver)

avoir des atomes crochus (French) to really hit it off (literally, to have hooked atoms)

Mouth relaxation

Comes the magic moment when the mental can at last become physical:

oxsanïstïr (Khakas, Siberia) to let oneself be kissed
conk (Hindi) the imprint of a kiss
smirikin (Scots) a stolen kiss
şap şap öpmek (Turkish) to kiss by making a smacking noise with the lips
csókolgat (Hungarian) to shower with kisses
cupang (Indonesian) a love bite (literally, Siamese fighting fish)

Spider feet

Then how easy life can be:

afilar (Argentinian Spanish) to chat with your sweetheart
gemas (Indonesian) a feeling of finding something or somebody so cute that you want to squeeze or pinch it
cafuné (Brazilian Portuguese) the loving, tender running of one's fingers through the hair of one's mate (from the act of a favoured slave who picked lice out of the slavemaster's child's hair)
cwtch (Welsh) to hug and snuggle up in a loving way
faire des pattes d'araignée (French) to touch lightly with the fingertips (literally, to make spider feet)

The Paraguayan way

One thing leads to another and soon events move to a whole new level. As the Russians say, '**Snyavshi shtany, po volosam ne gladyat**', once you've taken off your pants it's too late to look at your hair:

zulana (Mambwe, Zambia) to undress one another
lapóng (Tagalog, Philippines) sexual foreplay with the breasts
ikibari (Japanese) a lively needle, if a man is willing but
  under-endowed
Notstandt (German) an emergency erection
hacerlo a la paraguaya (Chilean Spanish) to have sex standing up (literally, the Paraguayan way)
voir la feuille à l'envers (French) to have sex under a tree
  (literally, to see the leaf from underneath)
rabu hoteru (Japanese) hotels especially for making love

The little death

The Maguindanaon language of the Philippines uses the same word, **lembu**, to describe both an orgasm and the fat of animals, whereas descriptions in other languages dwell on the intensity of the experience:

şiddetli heyecan (Turkish) literally, drastic excitement
höchste Wallung (German) literally, maximum bubbling

Secrets and lies

Such compelling activity brings with it, in some societies, a whole new set of excitements and problems:

Fensterln (German) the act of climbing a ladder to a woman's window, bypassing the parents and chaperones, to have sex in the night

besengkayau (Iban, Sarawak and Brunei) to hang by the hands from a beam and move along it hand over hand (done by young men courting at night to avoid walking on the springy and creaking floor)

miàla màndry (Malagasy, Madagascar) to spend the night away from home and yet be back in the early morning as if never having been away

un petit cinq-à-sept (French) a quick five to seven o'clock (an afternoon quickie with your lover before going home to your spouse)

In Rome love will come to you suddenly

Palindromes – words and sentences that read the same forwards and backwards – have been popular since ancient times. The Germans have even come up with a palindromic word – **Eibohphobie** – that means a fear of palindromes:

a dyma'r addewid diweddar am y da (Welsh) and here is the recent promise about the livestock

socorram-me, subi no onibus em Marrocos (Portuguese) help me I took a bus in Morocco

Selmas lakserøde garagedøre skal samles (Danish) Selma's salmon red garage doors must be assembled

ein Neger mit Gazelle zagt im Regen nie (German) a Negro with a gazelle never despairs in the rain

Roma tibi subito motibus ibit amor (Latin) in Rome love will come to you suddenly

Thanks for the treat

In Japan, **norokeru** means to boast in an annoying way about your great relationship, while **gochisosama** is a sarcastic reply (literally, thanks for the treat). But good, bad or too-perfect-to-be-true, in reality relationships come in all varieties:

sarbo (Dutch) a person who regularly sleeps with the same partner while living separately

nanoua (Gilbertese, Oceania) a heart divided between two loves

kutzwagers (Dutch) two or more men who have slept with the same woman

stroitel' (Russian) a man who likes to have sex with two women at the same time

Fried fish enthusiasm

The Germans have come up with some very useful descriptions of the nuances of modern love:

die Bettgeschichte a one-night stand (literally, bedtime story)

das Bratkartoffelverhältnis someone who cooks and cleans in exchange for occasional affection (literally, home-fries affair)

Lückenfüller the person one dates between two serious relationships (literally, hole-filler)

Backfischschwärmerei the crush young teenage girls get for older men (literally, fried fish enthusiasm)

Faded tomatoes

Relationships come in all lengths too. If it's not going to end in marriage or a seemly long-term partnership without legal ties, there inevitably must come the brutal moment when one has to tell the other that things are no longer rosy in the garden of love:

Trennungsagentur (German) a man hired by women to break the news to their men that they are dumped (literally, separation agent)

dejar clavado a alguien (Spanish) to dump someone, to stand them up (literally, to leave someone nailed)

dostat kopačky (Czech) to be dumped (literally, to get football boots)

dar calabazas (Spanish) to jilt, ignore or stand someone up; to reject a marriage proposal (literally, to give pumpkins)

il due di picche (Italian) to be dumped (literally, the two of spades, as in the card you are given)

proshla mlyubov' zavyali pomidory (Russian) the love affair is over (literally, love is gone, the tomatoes have faded)

Once bitten, twice shy

el gato escaldado del agua caliente huye (Spanish) the cat
that has been scalded runs away from hot water

sütten ağizi yanan yoğurdu üfleyerek yer (Turkish) if hot
milk burns your mouth, you'll blow the yoghurt before you
eat it

brændt barn skyer ilden (Danish) a burned child is shy of
fire

**puganaya vorona kusta/telezhnogo skripa/sobstvennoj
teni/boitsya** (Russian) a spooked crow is afraid of a bush/a
carriage wheel's squeak/its own shadow

mtafunwa na nyoka akiona unyasi hushtuka (Swahili)
one who has been bitten by a snake startles at a reed

cão picado por cobra, tem medo de linguiça (Portuguese)
a dog that has been bitten by a snake fears sausages

7.
Family Ties

žena se plaši prvog muža, a muž
se plaši druge žene (*Serbian*)
a wife is frightened of her first husband;
a husband is frightened of his second wife

Matchmaking

Until relatively recently in the West, open relationships of a pre-marital kind were not the norm. The Dutch described unmarried couples who lived together as **hokken**, literally, living in a pigsty together. In many other parts of the world such a set-up still wouldn't even be considered. The aim of society is to get a man and woman up the aisle, round the fire, or over the threshold:

gökyüzünde düğün var deseler, kadınlar merdiven kurmaya kalkar (Turkish proverb) if they say there is a wedding in the sky, women will try to put up a ladder

giftekniv (Norwegian) a person trying to get two people married

xem mat (Vietnamese) to see a candidate bride before deciding on the marriage

dulang (Manobo, Philippines) to arrange an auspicious marriage, especially between members of two opposing factions in order to bring about peace

sunkiya (Pali, India) the price paid for a wife

Objecting

Not that the young people in question always agree:

tlatlavala (Tsonga, South Africa) to refuse to marry the person selected for one by the family

kestë'shâétkë' (Mingo, USA) to object to a marriage

luyam (Manobo, Philippines) to hide one's true intentions in order to throw someone off guard so that one's real wishes can be carried out (for example, a girl who has resisted efforts to have her married then seems to change her mind so that she will not be watched, and she is thus able to run away)

Camel life

For women, at least, society could always hold the threat that they would end up alone:

ntingitihomu (Tsonga, South Africa) a girl that nobody wishes to marry

momá'kó'éné (Cheyenne, USA) having red eyes from crying because one's boyfriend got married to someone else

kurisumasu keiki (Japanese) leftover Christmas cake (traditionally applied to women over twenty-five years old)

quedar(se) a (para) vestir santos (Latin American Spanish) to be left unmarried (literally, to be left to dress figures of saints)

radudaraifu (Japanese) single women who spend much of their weekends cooking food and deep-freezing it so that it can be reheated in a hurry when they return late from work (literally, camel life)

gattara (Italian) a woman, often old and lonely, who devotes herself to stray cats

Old hat

In France the expression for an unmarried woman was even backed up by a festival. **Coiffer Sainte Catherine** meant to remain single after the age of twenty-five (literally, to put a headdress on St Catherine). From the Middle Ages, St Catherine has traditionally been the patron saint of young girls. On 25 November each year, girls would make beautiful headdresses to decorate statues of the saint. Unmarried women over twenty-five would attend a dance, wearing hats that they had made specially for the occasion, while everyone around wished them a rapid end to their spinsterhood.

Bare branches

However, since the implementation of the Chinese 'one child' policy things are changing in one part of the world at least:

>   **gagung** (Cantonese) a man who has no woman because of the inequality of the gender ratio (literally, bare branches)

False friends

chosen (Yiddish) bridegroom
dig in (Armenian) wife
fear (Irish) man
he (Hebrew) she
mama (Hindi) uncle
self (Egyptian Arabic) brother-in-law
that (Vietnamese) wife

Stalker

Of course, in all societies there have always been determined suitors:

> **baling** (Manobo, Philippines) the action of an unmarried
> woman who, when she wants to marry a certain man,
> goes to his house and refuses to leave until the marriage is
> agreed upon
>
> **nusukaaktuat** (Iñupiat, Inuit) grabbing a wife, ensuring
> marriage by capturing her

Regular footing

There are all kinds of reasons why people want to tie the knot:

> **se ranger** (French) to get married for domestic comfort and
> put life on a regular footing
>
> **ikabaebae** (Gilbertese, Oceania) to be engaged from
> childhood
>
> **damoz** (Amharic, Ethiopia) a temporary marriage arrange-
> ment, usually for pay, between a man who is away on his
> travels and a woman who is his companion or cook
>
> **casar(se) con hombre en base** (Latin American Spanish) to
> get married when you're already pregnant

Wedding lists

Female relatives of the Swahili groom perform a ritual called **kupeka begi** (send a bag) in which they bring to the bride gifts from her husband. In response, the bride's female relations perform **kupeka mswaki** (bring the chewsticks), whereby they deliver to the groom a tray of toiletries. This is particularly important because the bride and groom are forbidden to meet before marriage.

The bride wore black

In the Tsonga language of South Africa **qanda** refers to the traditional bringing of an ox along with the bride as a symbol or guarantee of her future progeny. The ox is then eaten by her new husband's family. She is not allowed to see any part of it; if she does she should say, 'They killed my child.' If language is our evidence, this is by no means the weirdest wedding event in the world:

trá-hôn (Vietnamese) to substitute another girl for the bride
faanifin maanoo (Mandinka, West Africa) a bride wearing black (signifying that she had sex with her future husband before the ceremony)
ii/fuya (Ndonga, Namibia) strips of meat from the wedding ox wound around the arm of the bridesmaid
infar-cake (Scots) a cake broken over the bride's head as she crosses the threshold of her new home

Apron strings

Wives come in all styles:

ntshadi (Setswana, Botswana) a dear little wife

mon cinquante-pour-cent (French) wife (literally, my fifty per cent)

sokozuma (Japanese) a woman who settles for a so-so marriage just to get it out of the way

minekokon (Japanese) a woman who gives up a high-powered job in the city for a dull life in the country with a quiet husband

As do husbands:

mandilon (Mexican Spanish) a hen-pecked, oppressed husband (from **mandil** meaning apron)

stroin (Bengali) a married man who does everything and anything his wife says

tøffelhelt (Norwegian) someone who has nothing to say in a marriage or at home (literally, slipper hero)

mariteddu tamant'è un ditu lèddu voli essa rivaritu (Corsican proverb) a husband must be respected, even if he's very short

Green hat

We can only hope that neither of them has an urge to misbehave:

piniscar la uva (Chilean Spanish) to seduce a woman who's already taken (literally, to grab the grape)

fanifikifihana (Malagasy, Madagascar) a charm for making another man's wife disliked by her husband, or the husband by the wife

dài lümào (Chinese) implies that someone's wife is unfaithful (literally, wearing a green hat)

kentenga (Tsonga, South Africa) to find oneself suddenly without some vital item (said of a man whose only wife has run away, or when the roof of a hut has blown off)

Recognized

Though sometimes such potentially destructive liaisons can be defused by being formalized:

kutua-na (Yamana, Chile) to give the second wife the place of the first in the wigwam

cicisbeo (Italian) an acknowledged lover of a married woman

chandek (Malay) a recognized concubine of a prince (as distinct from **gundek**, an inferior wife, or **jamah-jamahan**, a casual mistress)

antis (Manobo, Philippines) a father's action, after his daughter's adultery, when he gives his son-in-law another daughter as a second wife

Three's a crowd

In some societies, of course, monogamy doesn't even exist as an ideal, throwing up a whole new set of complications:

lefufa (Setswana, Botswana) the jealousy between the wives of one man

elungan (Manobo, Philippines) to divide one's time equally between two wives who live in separate households

gintawan (Manobo, Philippines) the energy and industry of the first wife (when her husband takes an additional wife) as a result of the competition from the second wife

allupaareik (Iñupiat, Inuit) the return of a woman after a wife exchange

Hope springs eternal

In these days of **rikonmiminenzo** (Japanese), the divorce-promotion generation, things are never that simple in any case:

manàntom-bàdy (Malagasy, Madagascar) to put away a wife without divorcing her altogether

gila talak (Malay) a husband or wife who are divorced yet wishing very much to reunite

ebpamituanen (Maguindanaon, Philippines) a divorced person who keeps their figure in the hope of a future marriage

china buta (Malay) the intermediate husband a divorced Muslim woman must have before remarriage to her original husband

Workbox or housewife

Various languages have words with surprising double meanings, creating some thought-provoking associations:

mjall (Swedish) dandruff or tender
varik (Buli, Ghana) castrated or huge and strong
váram (Tamil) friendship or a week
dánamu (Telugu, India) a gift or elephant semen
ola (Samoan) fishing basket or life
panjitkori (Korean) workbox or housewife
turba (Italian) crowd or trouble
toil (Mongolian) mirror or dictionary
rooie (Dutch) carrots or ginger
saje (Hausa, Nigeria) side whiskers or a sergeant
hege' (Hebrew) steering wheel or murmur

Relative values

Let's look on the bright side. Though often derided in our fickle age, family life can bring many and varied benefits:

agusto (Latin American Spanish) the cosiness felt when snuggling with a relative

onimagu (Yamana, Chile) to feel such pity as relatives do towards each other when hurt

ka-otaba (Gilbertese, Oceania) to preserve the beauty and freshness of a daughter-in-law

dyadya (Russian) a rich relative abroad, considered as a source of money (literally, an uncle)

bombela (Tsonga, South Africa) to make free with another's belongings (especially with those of one's maternal uncle)

Dirt on the nest

Although those who hold up the family as the answer to all things are probably sadly deluded:

butika roko (Gilbertese, Oceania) a brother-in-law coming around too often

kyodai-genka (Japanese) a fight or argument between siblings

mātrigāmī (Hindi) one who commits incest with his mother

Nestbeschmutzer (German) someone ruining the reputation of the family or community (literally, someone who puts dirt on the nest)

rihorhabodo (Tsonga, South Africa) an irresponsible man who does not care for his family, but just roams around, generally in town

wićawokha (Dakota, USA) a man who lives with his wife's relations (literally, a buried man)

bayram değil (seyran değil enişte beni niye öptü?) (Turkish proverb) there must be something behind this (literally, it's not festival time, it's not a pleasure trip, so why did my brother-in-law kiss me?)

Congo confusion

As every son-in-law knows, you've got to be very careful what you say about one particular family member. In the Lokele language of the Congo there is only a tonal difference (shown by the capital letters) between **aSOolaMBA boili**, I'm watching the riverbank, and **aSOoLAMBA boIli**, I'm boiling my mother-in-law.

Auntie

In the Pakistani language of Urdu a woman is addressed in the following way:

apa (or **baji**)	by her younger sisters or brothers
khala	by her sister's children
mani (or **momani**)	by the children of her husband's sisters
ch' hachi	by the children of her husband's younger brothers
ta'i	by the children of her husband's elder brothers
p' huppi	by the children of her brother
bahu	by her parents-in-law
nani	by the children of her daughters
dadi	by the children of her sons
bhabi	by her sisters-in-law and brothers-in-law
patiji	by her aunts and uncles
sas	by her daughter-in-law
nand	by her brother's wife
sali	by the husband of her sister

Prodigal son

In Fiji, they observe the custom of **vasu** which gives a son certain powers over his mother's native place. He may take anything he covets from the houses, tear down the fruit trees, and generally behave in such a way that if he were a stranger he would be clubbed to death.

Family tree

Of course, however much you try to escape the familial bond, there's really no getting away from who you are and where you're from:

asal pagasal (Maguindanaon, Philippines) to trace family relationships among people newly acquainted with each other

anestolt (Norwegian) proud of one's ancestors

progonoplexia (Greek) bragging about one's ancestors

kupu (Hawaiian) one whose ancestors were born where he himself was born

kacang lupakan kulit (Malay) a man who refuses to acknowledge his background and forgets his family or friends once he has made a fortune for himself

IDIOMS OF THE WORLD

Between the devil and the deep blue sea

telan mati emak, luah mati bapa (Malay) if you swallow it
your mother will die, if you throw it up your father will die

estar entre a espada e a parede (Portuguese) to be between
the sword and the wall

tussen twee vuren staan (Dutch) to be between two fires

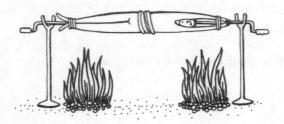

byt mezhdu molotom i nakovalnyei (Russian) between
hammer and anvil

wählen zwischen Hölle und Fegefeuer (German) to choose
between hell and purgatory

se correr o bicho pega e se ficar o bicho (Portuguese) if
you run, the animal will catch you, if you stay it will eat you

eddyr daa stoyl ta toyn er laare (Manx, Isle of Man) between
two stools your arse is on the floor

8.
Kids

ogni scarafone è bello a mamma sua
(*Italian*)
every mother likes her own beetle

Pragmatic future

When it comes to the prospect of having children, the Japanese have brought the vocabulary firmly into the twenty-first century:

kondoumukeikaku the way in which some women over thirty-five have unprotected sex with strangers to have children

nakayoshi ninpu (buddy pregnancy) describes the act of two women deliberately getting pregnant at the same time so that they can experience childbirth together (literally, pregnancy-now plan)

shoshika a future society without children

Warped

From the moment a woman conceives, a new life has begun – for the one in the womb, obviously, but also for the mother. French metaphors take particular notice of her difference in appearance: she has **tombée sur un clou rouillé**, fallen on a rusty nail, and thus swollen; or, to put it another way, she has begun **gondoler sur la devanture**, to warp from the display window:

ubháya-siras (Sanskrit) two-headed, a pregnant female
ajamonarse (Spanish) used to describe a pregnant woman's increase in size (literally, to be like a ham)
proglotit' arbouz (Russian) to become pregnant (literally, to swallow a watermelon)

Longings

She starts to feel differently too:

    dohada (Sanskrit) the longing of a pregnant woman for particular objects

    afa-dratsiaina (Malagasy, Madagascar) the condition of a pregnant woman who has eaten what she had a great longing for

A mark of frustration

When a Maltese pregnant woman has a wish, one should try to satisfy her, or else the baby will be born with a large mole on its face; this is known as **it-tebgħa tax-xewqa**, the wish mark.

Paternity leave

In some African tribes the men will take to their beds for the entire duration of their wife's pregnancy, while the women continue to work as usual until a few hours before giving birth. This is called **couvade** (from the French word meaning, literally, brooding or hatching). The men believe that they are cleverer and stronger than women and so are better able to defend unborn children against evil spirits. Prone in his bed, the husband simulates the pains that the wife actually undergoes. Following the birth of the child, he keeps to his bed and receives all the attentions which in other societies are bestowed upon the mother. Variations of this behaviour have been seen in such diverse places as Papua New Guinea, Bolivia and the Basque districts of Northern Spain and South-West France.

Those who comes divided

The Fon people of Benin are particularly enthusiastic about twins. All twins are regarded as separate parts of a single being so their birth signals the arrival of **mabassa**, those who comes divided. They also believe that some babies may refuse to be born. Just before birth, the elder of a set of twins is said to peek out of the womb to survey the outside world. If it determines that the world is unsafe, it returns to the womb to report to its sibling. The twins may then refuse their delivery. If one twin dies, a small wooden image of the deceased must be carried by the mother and cared for at all times. All gifts to the survivor must be duplicated: one for the living twin and one for the dead.

kœmœ (Chewa, South East Africa) the firstborn twin

embangurane (Kiga Nkore, Niger-Congo) twins of different sex

Breast water

Caring for a helpless baby has inspired some charming words around the world:

komvya (Mambwe, Zambia) to feed a child with one's finger

namaonga (Gilbertese, Oceania) to taste a little portion and chew it for a baby

ukkun (Sinhala, Sri Lanka) an expression of fondness used to infants when breastfeeding

anoka (Malagasy, Madagascar) the perfect contentment in sucking or drinking (used primarily of children or the young of animals at the breast)

ngibá (Tagalog, Philippines) a baby's tendency to cry when held by a stranger

We will rock you

In Southern Africa they certainly have ways and means of keeping a baby quiet:

kolopeka (Mambwe, Zambia) to appease a child, stop him from crying by amusing him

vundzata (Tsonga, South Africa) to turn a child's head sideways when on its mother's back or when put to sleep

pakatika (Mambwe, Zambia) to place one's own child on the lap of a companion

khan'wetela (Tsonga, South Africa) to rock a child to sleep on one's back by nudging with the elbows

halalata (Tsonga, South Africa) to throw a baby up into the air, at a ceremony of the first new moon after its birth

wo-mba (Bakweri, Cameroon) the smiling in sleep by children

Babygrow

Aꜰʟʟ too soon the little creature wants to go its own way:

abula (Setswana, Botswana) the attempt of a baby to move when lying on its belly

toto-toto (Setswana, Botswana) a term of endearment to encourage a baby to stand or walk

a'matiti (Rotuman, South Pacific) to accustom a baby to cooler temperatures by taking it on a walk in the early morning

dede (Swahili) to stand uncertainly, as a child just beginning to walk stands when not held

sparkedragt (Danish) a pair of rompers (literally, kicking suit)

kopisata (Yamana, Chile) to get thin, like a fat baby when it gets older

Draggling

Dᴇsᴘɪᴛᴇ its best intentions, it's still a long way from being independent:

ma-ma (Car, Nicobar Islands) 'father', 'daddy', the child's cry for its father

po-po (Car, Nicobar Islands) 'mother', 'mummy', the child's cry for its mother

upuss-eata (Yamana, Chile) to draggle after one, as a child, a long line or anything tied to a string

pobi (Buli, Ghana) to wrap or to tie a child on one's back

n-velekula (Kerewe, Tanzania) to swing a child round from the back to hip, preparatory to putting it down or feeding it

A desk job

In Malta, the baby's first year is regarded as dangerous, so the first birthday – **Il-Quccija** – is a happy event. On this day the child's future is suggested when a tray of small objects is carried in and placed on the floor. The baby is then put down and allowed to crawl in any direction it wants. What it picks up from the tray signifies its future. The traditional objects include an egg (**bajda**) for an abundance of happiness, a pen (**pinna**) for a desk job, some coins (**muniti**) for wealth, a ball (**ballun**) for sport, rosary beads (**kuruna**) for the church, scissors (**mqass**) for tailoring, a book (**ktieb**) for a lawyer, a hammer (**martell**) for a carpenter, and these days other items such as a stethoscope (for a doctor) or a CD (for a disc jockey).

Mother love

As the Nigerian saying goes, **nwanyi umu iri o dighi ihe mere nabali o naghi ama**, when a woman has ten children there is nothing that happens in the night that she does not know about:

wahdećapi (Dakota, USA) the sympathy that is said to exist between a mother and her absent children, producing peculiar sensations in the breast

songkom (Malay) to bury the face in a mother's lap (as a child)

xilandzalandza (Tsonga, South Africa) a child constantly staying close to its mother

Cuckoo

With all this vulnerability at stake, one can only pray for decent parents ...

kukushka (Russian) a mother who gives up her child to be raised by others (literally, a cuckoo)

kaelling (Danish) a woman who stands on the steps of her house yelling obscenities at her kids

Kinderfeindlichkeit (German) an intense dislike or disregard of children

---

False friends

taxi (Greek) classroom

Gymnasium (German) grammar school, high school

son (Vietnamese) to be still childless

Daughter in a box

… but not to the point where they overdo it:

onba-higasa (Japanese) a wealthy family's pampered child
(literally, wet nurse and parasol)

curlingforeldre (Danish) parents who do anything to sweep
the road of life ahead of their children to ensure that it is
free of obstacles (literally, curling parents)

hakoiri-musume (Japanese) a young woman who has always
been protected from the harsh realities of life by doting
parents (literally, daughter in a box)

ser flor de estufa (Spanish) overprotected, not allowed to
become independent (literally, to be a hothouse flower)

Impossible child

'The child who is one night old,' say the Arabs, 'has already learned to annoy its parents.' It doesn't stop there:

lundaezi (Lozi, Niger-Congo) to walk in the manner of a disrespectful angry child

riu' (Iban, Sarawak and Brunei) rushing about and getting in the way (especially of children)

upuk'anaana (Yamana, Chile) to throw away anything cooked, as a naughty child might throw away a fish its mother gave it to eat

bunget (Manobo, Philippines) as a child, to want something one can't have, get angry and then refuse it when it is finally offered

Dolls' house

Distractions must be found; and the Yamana speakers of Chile have several delightfully specific words to describe the making of toys for children and how they play with them:

tukau-iyana to put a foot or feet on a doll or a picture of one

utellana to make or put eyes in the head of a figure one carves or draws

tumusgaia to put down with the face upwards, as with some dolls on a table

kaiyena-na to play quietly, as a little child with a toy

manax-soatekana to play with someone else's toys

Junken a munken

But who needs toys when kids are so delightfully inventive anyway?

goagoana (Setswana, Botswana) to shout at each other in play

chottu (Tamil) a slap on the head with both hands in play

ha-lo-po (Car, Nicobar Islands) to have practical jokes played on one

junken a munken, a sucka sucka po, wailuku wailuku, bum bum show (Hawaiian Pidgin) a kids' way of deciding who goes first: eeny meeny miney mo

Cheese head

The years race by; things seem to change so fast:

propanach (Gaelic) a well-built boy, beginning to run about

botshegangangatswane (Setswana, Botswana) little boys when still at a stage when they are unabashed by their nakedness

kaaskop (Dutch) a very blond, rosy-cheeked child (literally, cheese head)

timtum (Yiddish) a beardless youth with a high-pitched voice

My sister's toenails look like my grandfather's

From 'Around the rugged rock, the ragged rascal ran' to 'red leather, yellow leather', a key part of learning a language is being able to master its tongue-twisters. They are always decidedly odd sentences. One French example featuring the s sound focuses on food:

Combien de sous sont ces saucissons-ci? Ces saucissons-ci sont six sous (How much are these sausages here? These sausages here are six cents.)

While a German tongue-twister that offers a lot of practice in the pronunciation of sch portrays a rather dangerous situation:

Zwei schwartze schleimige Schlangen sitzen zwischen zwei spitzigen Steinen und zischen (Two black slimy snakes sit between two pointed stones and hiss.)

Other favourites include:

Kuku kaki kakak kakak ku kayak kuku kaki kakek kakek ku (Indonesian) My sister's toenails look like my grandfather's.

Méla babka v kapse brabce, brabec babce v kapse píp. Zmáčkla babka brabce v kapse, brabec babce v kapse chcíp (Czech) Grandma had a sparrow in her pocket and the sparrow made a sound. Grandma pressed the sparrow and it died.

Als vliegen achter vliegen vliegen, vliegen vliegen vliegensvlug (Dutch) If flies fly behind flies, flies will fly like lightning.

Król Karol kupił Królowej Karolinie korale koloru koralowego (Polish) King Karl bought Queen Caroline a coral-coloured bead.

Saya sebal sama situ sebab situ suka senyum-senyum sama suami saya saya sehingga sekarang suami saya suka senyum-senyum sendiri sembari sama (Indonesian) I hate you because you used to smile at my husband; now he likes to smile for no obvious reason when he is with me.

Far, får får får? Nej, inte får får får, får får lamm (Swedish) Father, do sheep have sheep? No, sheep don't have sheep, sheep have lambs.

Kan-jang-kong-jang kong-jang-jang-eun kang kong-jang-jang-ee-go, dwen-jang-kong-jang kong-jang-jang-eun kong kong-jang-jang-ee-da (Korean) The president of the soy-sauce factory is president Kang and the president of the bean-paste factory is president Kong.

Learning curve

Soon enough it's time to start getting to grips with the ways and means of the adult world ...

kinder-vraag (Dutch) a childish question

ABC-Schuetze (German) a pupil in the first year of school (literally, ABC shooter)

skolplikt (Swedish) compulsory school attendance

managòana (Malagasy, Madagascar) to go over a list of names to see if all are there

ageographetos (Greek) useless at geography

katapádama (Sinhala, Sri Lanka) a lesson committed to memory

chongak (Malay) to raise the head and the chin or to do mental arithmetic in class

daoshu (Chinese) to count backwards

sonkkopta (Korean) to count on one's fingers

mushtiya (Sinhala, Sri Lanka) a fist, a closed hand (also applied to the behaviour of a teacher who withholds some knowledge from his pupils through fear that they may surpass him)

Target practice

... with all the unpleasant ordeals that that entails:

quemarse las pestanas (cejas) (Spanish) to study hard
  (literally, to burn one's eyelashes (eyebrows))

nochnoe (Russian) late-night studying, as before exams

acordeón (Mexican Spanish) a crib sheet used to cheat in a
  test or exam (literally, an accordion)

ponchar (Cuban Spanish) to fail an exam (literally, to get a
  flat tyre)

vo chuoi (Vietnamese) to fail an exam (literally, to slip on a
  banana skin)

kvarsittare (Swedish) a pupil who has not been moved up

suberidome (Japanese) a school one applies to in case one
  isn't accepted elsewhere (literally, skid stopper)

Hanging out

What every parent fears is **slynaldern** (Swedish), the awkward
age, when their once innocent and biddable child starts rebelling
against their authority:

kutu embun (Malay) on the streets constantly; young people
  who roam the streets at night

hangjongeren* (Dutch) groups of teenagers with nothing
  to do but hang around in groups, making strange grunting
  noises at passers-by (literally, hanging youth)

katoro buaka (Gilbertese, Oceania) neglectful of one's
  parents or grandparents

---

* Obviously, not to be confused with **hangouderen** (Dutch), pensioners who have nothing
to do but hang around in considerable numbers in shopping malls and hamburger bars
(literally, hanging elderly)

Filial

The good parent can only hope that all their love and hard work is reciprocated:

matteyyatā (Pali, India) filial love towards one's mother
tindi (Tsonga, South Africa) to express joy at seeing one's parents (of children)
chengqi (Chinese) to grow up to be a useful person

IDIOMS OF THE WORLD

Like father like son

kakov pop takov i prikhod (Russian) like priest like church
æblet falder ikke langt fra stamen (Danish) the apple doesn't fall far from the trunk
ibn al bat 'awwam (Arabic) the son of a duck is a floater
filho de peixe sabe nadar (Portuguese) a fish's child knows how to swim
de tal palo tal astilla (Spanish) from such stick comes such splinter
hijo de tigre sale rayado (Central American Spanish) the son of the tiger turns out striped
barewa tayi gudu danta ya yi rarrafe? (Hausa, Nigeria) how can the offspring of a gazelle crawl when its mother is a fast runner?

9.
Body Beautiful

kozla boysya speredi, konya — szadi, a likhogo cheloveka — so vsekh storon (*Russian*)
beware of the goat from its front side, of the horse — from its back side, and the evil man — from any side

Mugshot

Our face is our fortune, they say, but some are undeniably more fortunate than others:

chimmurui no kao (Japanese) a face that would stop a clock
kwabbig (Dutch) flabby pendulous cheeks
oriiti (Anywa, Nilo-Saharan) wrinkles on the forehead
papada (Spanish) a double chin
boirg (Gaelic) a small screwed-up mouth
busachd (Gaelic) the deformity of blubber-lips
bemandromba (Malagasy, Madagascar) having a large and
    ill-looking head
**avoir un oeil qui joue au billard et l'autre qui compte
    les points** (French) said of someone who is cross-eyed (liter-
    ally, to have one eye that's playing billiards while the other
    is off counting the points)

False friends

ache (Bashgali, India) an eye
bonk (Dutch) bone
flint (Swedish) bald head
glad (Dutch) smooth, sleek
groin (French) snout
honk (Armenian) eyebrow
mute (Latvian) mouth
pea (Estonian) head
pong (Khowar, Pakistan) foot

Gobstruck

Of course it's all too easy to spoil the appearance of what we've been given …

vaaye-nokke (Malayalam) to stare at somebody with your mouth open (literally, mouth-see)

gaillseach (Gaelic) a large mouthful which makes the cheeks bulge out

… especially if we're putting it to good use:

kecomak-kecamik (Indonesian) to move the mouth around when eating something or saying a prayer

fújtat (Hungarian) to pant, puff and blow

menggonggong (Malay) to carry something in your mouth

ayapsun (Dakota, USA) to pull something out by the roots using the mouth

raspakhivat' varezhky (Russian) to drop one's jaw in surprise or amazement (literally, to open someone's mitten)

Lippy

With the fleshiest part of that useful opening, emotion can easily get the better of appearance:

maiskuttaa (Finnish) to smack one's lips

bibidia (Swahili) to thrust out and turn down the lower lip as a sign of derision or contempt

Tsk tsk

In many parts of the world, the tongue is not used just for speaking or eating:

tam-tac (Vietnamese) to smack the tongue as a sign of admiration

mitimiti (Rapa Nui, Easter Island) to click one's tongue as a sign of disagreement or of annoyance (tsk, tsk)

auau (Bugotu, Solomon Islands) to stick the tongue out

lamz (Persian) rolling the tongue about the mouth to pick the teeth

imel-es (Ik, Nilo-Saharan) to move the tongue in and out like a snake

Trouble gum

Americans talk disparagingly of 'English teeth', but England is not the only country in the world where dental radiance could be improved:

kasyápa (Sanskrit) having black teeth

kadadat (Sinhala, Sri Lanka) possessing only half of your original teeth

wahdatepa (Dakota, USA) to wear one's own teeth short

si gwa pau (Cantonese) someone with buck teeth (literally, watermelon shoveller)

Smiling, squirting, stripping

The Italians say, 'Teeth placed before the tongue give good advice'; and whatever your gnashers look like, you can always put them to good use:

gigil (Tagalog, Philippines) the gritting of the teeth when controlling emotion

n'wayin'wayi (Tsonga, South Africa) to smile showing the teeth

ntseka (Tsonga, South Africa) to squirt forcibly through the teeth

ki'it (Manobo, Philippines) to bite off something with the front teeth (as when eating corn on the cob)

yigul-a (Yamana, Chile) to pull out stitches with the teeth

eeti (Rapanui, Easter Island) to strip off bark or hard skin with the teeth

dona (Yamana, Chile) to take out lice from a person's head and squash them between one's teeth

dentilegus (Latin) one who picks up his teeth after they have been knocked out

Long teeth

When the French talk of aiming for the impossible, they say they are trying to **prendre la lune avec les dents**, literally, to seize the moon with one's teeth; to be very ambitious, likewise, is **avoir les dents qui rayent le parquet**, to have teeth that scratch the floor. For the Finns, to do something unwillingly is **pitkin hampain**, with long teeth; while for the Spanish, **andar con el diente largo**, walking around with long teeth, means to be very hungry.

Copping an eyeful

'The eyes are the mirror of the soul,' say the Japanese, echoing an English saying. But often it's the more mundane aspects of these organs that people worry about:

xitsavatsava (Tsonga, South Africa) the involuntary twitching of an eyelid or eyebrow

bitlisisa (Setswana, Botswana) a sore eye that has been rubbed

kuseng (Manobo, Philippines) to rub one's eyes with the back of the hand

rabun ayam (Malay) poor eyesight, especially during sunset

Bewitching

As with the teeth, our peepers are at their best when they're put to use:

gwilgat (Breton, France) to watch from the corner of one's eye
langut (Malay) to look upwards longingly
pangangalumbabà (Tagalog, Philippines) a pensive look
  (with the head supported by the palm)
ingikaranawá (Sinhala, Sri Lanka) to wink significantly
vekaveka (Luvale, Zambia) the shiftiness of eyes, looking here
  and there with madness or evil intent
temuna (Luvale, Zambia) to pull down an eyelid in mockery
embila (Maguindanaon, Philippines) to pretend to be
  cross-eyed

Cyrano

The French say that 'a big nose never spoiled a handsome face', a charitable judgement, perhaps influenced by the many fine probosci to be found in that country. But others have more serious problems than mere size:

khuranásá (Sinhala, Sri Lanka) one having a nose like a
  horse's hoof
tapíl (Tagalog, Philippines) flat-nosed
bapp-nose (Scots) a nose threatening to meet the chin
ngongò (Tagalog, Philippines) one who talks with a twang
  due to a nasal disorder
patināsikā (Pali, India) a false nose

Lughole

Big or small, flat or sticky-out, our final external organs on the head are also closely observed by our worldwide languages:

anak telinga (Malay) the external gristly portion of the ear
budálu (Telugu, India) the place where the top of the ear meets the head
ukkanna (Pali, India) having the ears erect
n'wii (Tsonga, South Africa) to have buzzing in the ears, as when under water
parece Volkswagen con las puertas abiertas (Latin American Spanish) big-eared (literally, he looks like a Volkswagen with the doors open)

Grass belong head

In the Tok Pisin language of Papua New Guinea, they call hair **gras bilong het**. Such grass may take different forms, quite apart from appearing in all the wrong places:

kesuir (Malay) hairy nostrils
gejigeji-mayuge (Japanese) bushy eyebrows (literally, centi-pede eyebrows)
giri-giri (Hawaiian Pidgin) the place where two or three hairs stick up no matter what
mas (Hindi) soft hair appearing above a lad's upper lip, heralding the imminent advent of youth
kapúcchala (Sanskrit) a tuft of hair on the hind part of the head (hanging down like a tail)
pédevádu (Telugu, India) a man upon whose face hair does not grow

Octopus monk

For many men age brings a related and inescapable problem:

katok (Russian) a bald patch (literally, a skating rink)

baakoodo hage (Japanese) said of a man with receding hair who combs what remains at the sides over the top of his head (literally, barcode bald, due to how it looks viewed from above)

hlohlwe (Tsonga, South Africa) a forehead with corners devoid of hair (applied to a person whose hair is receding)

tako-nyudo (Japanese) a baldy (literally, octopus monk)

Oeuf-tête

The French, in particular, have a fine range of expressions for this challenging condition:

avoir le melon déplumé to have a plucked melon
avoir une boule de billard to have a billiard ball
ne plus avoir de cresson sur la cafetière no longer to have
  watercress on the coffeepot
ne plus avoir de gazon sur la platebande no longer to
  have a lawn on the flowerbed

avoir la casquette en peau de fesses to have a cap made
  out of buck skin
être chauve comme un genou to be as bald as a knee
avoir un vélodrome à mouches to have a velodrome for
  flies

Well-armed

We have upper and lower arms and elbows, but the Swedes have a word for the opposite side of the arm from the elbow – **armveck**. Other useful words stress the practical uses of these appendages:

kwapatira (Chichewa, Malawi) to carry something tucked under the arm

cholat (Malay) to dig with the elbow or the hand

athevotho (Bugotu, Solomon Islands) to swing the arms, wave or clear away smoke

Japanese birthdays

In the West, the birthdays that are particularly celebrated are those of coming of age: 18 and 21. In Japan, the older you get the more solemnly your birthday (**sanga**) is celebrated. The birthdays of especial importance are:

40: **shoro**, the beginning of old age, since Confucius said: 'When I was forty I did not wander.'

61: **kanreki**, the completion of the sixty-year cycle; the celebrant wears a red cap and a red kimono and is congratulated by everybody for having become 'a newborn baby once more'

70: **koki**, rare age, so called because the poet Tu Fu said that it was a privilege for a person to reach the age of seventy

77: **kiju**, long and happy life

88: **beiju**, the rice birthday

These last two birthdays gain their names from the similarity of the Japanese ideograms for 'joy' and 'rice' to those for the numbers 77 and 88 respectively.

Handy

In the Tsonga language of South Africa they have the expressive word **vunyiriri**, the stiffness of hands and feet felt on cold wintry mornings; while the Telugu language of India describes **kamikili**, the hand held with fingers bent and separated. However they're positioned, their uses are manifold:

apphoteti (Pali, India) to clap the hands as a sign of pleasure

aupiupiu (Mailu, Papua New Guinea) to flick an insect off the body

ka-cha-to-re (Car, Nicobar Islands) to hang down by one's hands

duiri (Buli, Ghana) to pass one's hands over skin so that the hairs stand up

pamamaywáng (Tagalog, Philippines) placing the hands on one's hips

geu (Bugotu, Solomon Islands) to thrust one's hand into a bag

And two are even better than one:

raup (Malay) to scoop up with both hands

anjali (Hindi) the cup-shaped hollow formed by joining the two palms together

chal (Car, Nicobar Islands) to lift up something heavy using both hands

kaf faksara (Rotuman, South Pacific) to clap the hands with one finger bent inwards to make a hollow sound

Digital

'Without fingers,' say the Moroccans, 'the hand would be a spoon.'
And where indeed would we be without our essential digits?

gamaza (Arabic) to take with the fingertips
gutól (Tagalog, Philippines) snipping with the fingernails
menonjolkan (Malay) to push one's fingers into someone's face
tstumi-oidagana (Yamana, Chile) to offer one's finger or any
    part of oneself to be bitten
sena (Sinhala, Sri Lanka) the time that elapses while snapping
    the thumb and forefinger ten times

Doigt de seigneur

In French, starting from the one nearest the thumb, you have **index**; **majeur** – biggest finger; **annulaire** – ring finger; and, last but not least, **auriculaire** – literally, the ear finger, because it's the only one small enough to stick in your ear. But if your digits don't stop there, you have to go to the Luvale language of Zambia for the **sambwilo**, the sixth finger or toe.

Expansive

In the Malay language, they use the space between the fingers for a series of useful measurements:

jengkal the span between thumb and finger
jengkul the span between thumb and index finger
telunjok the span between thumb and the joint of the bent
    index finger
ketengkeng the span between thumb and little finger

Classified

Further down the body, one reaches those parts generally described as private. In Southern Africa, they appear to have thought more than most about keeping it that way:

phindzela (Tsonga, South Africa) to cover one's private parts carefully

tswi (Tsonga, South Africa) to expose one's private parts by bending forward

ikokomela (Setswana, Botswana) to look at one's own private parts

Peppers and Parasols

The Japanese have a memorable vocabulary to describe their (male) genitalia:

imo a potato, a penis that is short and fat

tōgarashi a red pepper, a penis that is small and pink

gobō a burdock, a penis that is large and tubular

kenke small, tight testicles (literally pickles)

karakasa a paper parasol, a penis that is unusually top-heavy

Map of the world

French slang uses even more elaborate metaphors. A penis is either **une anguille de calecif**, an underwear eel, or **un cigare à moustache**, a cigar with a moustache. In similarly fanciful fashion, breasts are described as **une mappemonde**, literally, a map of the world (spread across two hemispheres).

Bum deal

Round the back, it seems, we are free to be frank, especially in East Africa and the Philippines:

shuri (Swahili) a person whose buttocks stick out more than those of the average person

tuwad (Maguindanaon, Philippines) to make one's buttocks project

egkisu-kisu (Maguindanaon, Philippines) to move the buttocks little by little

pinginyika (Swahili) to move the buttocks with a circular motion when walking or dancing

Milk bottles

When it comes to the legs, English has no word to describe the back of the knee. Irish Gaelic calls it the **ioscaid**, the Swedes **knäveck**, while the Native American Dakota language calls it **hunyoka-khmin**. Other languages are similarly descriptive about both the appearance and the movement of our lower half:

euischios (Ancient Greek) with beautiful hips

melkflessen (Dutch) bare legs which have not been sun-tanned (literally, milk bottles)

kerchiholl (Albanian) having thin lower legs

anyula (Tsonga, South Africa) to open one's legs indecently

hiza ga warau (Japanese) the wobbly feeling you have in your legs after dashing up several flights of stairs (literally, my knees are laughing)

Thin as a rake

When it comes to the whole package, there are differences of opinion about how substantial you should be. In general, the modern world applauds the skinny, even as our languages hark back to a less prosperous age in their comparisons:

ser magro como um palito (Portuguese) to be as thin as a toothpick

zo mager als een lat zijn (Dutch) to be as thin as a wooden latch

po ru zhu (Mandarin) thin as paper

flaco como un güin (Cuban Spanish) thin as a sugar-cane flower

kostur slab (Macedonian) thin as a skeleton

loksh (Yiddish) a noodle, a tall thin person

Bacon buoy

While fatties come in for all kinds of criticism:

vuthikithiki (Tsonga, South Africa) body fat which shakes at every step

juyaku-bara (Japanese) a paunch (literally, company director's stomach)

tivili (Sinhala, Sri Lanka) a person with three dents in his belly (from fatness)

foca (Spanish) a very fat woman (literally, a seal)

yongzhong (Chinese) too fat and clumsy to move

gordo como una buoya (Cuban Spanish) fat as a buoy

abspecken (German) losing weight (literally, de-baconing)

fai prima a saltargli sopra che girargli intorno (Italian) it's faster to jump on him than go round him (because he's so fat)

Illusory

Not, of course, that you can always judge from appearances:

Sitzriese (German) someone who is actually quite short but
looks tall when they're sitting down (literally, sitting giant)
edtiudan (Maguindanaon, Philippines) to pretend to be lame

IDIOMS OF THE WORLD

You cannot make a silk purse
out of a sow's ear

rozhdennyj polzat letat ne mozhet (Russian) if you're born
to crawl you can't fly
on ne peut faire d'une buse un épervier (French) you
can't turn a buzzard into a sparrowhawk
**al draagt een aap een gouden ring, het is en blijft een
lelijk ding** (Dutch) even if the monkey wears a golden ring
it remains ugly
fare le nozze con i fichi secchi (Italian) to celebrate a
wedding with dried figs

10.
Dressed to Kill

siku utakayokwenda uchi ndiyo siku
utakayokutana na mkweo (*Swahili*)
*the day you decide to leave your house naked is
the day you run into your in-laws*

A memorable smile

Whatever Nature has provided you with, you always have the chance to make your own improvements:

sulong (Iban, Sarawak and Brunei) to decorate the front teeth with gold (formerly brass)

nyin-susu (Bambara, West Africa) to blacken someone's gums for cosmetic purposes

pen bilong maus (Tok Pisin, Papua New Guinea) lipstick

False friends

Rock (German) skirt
veste (French) jacket
romp (Afrikaans) skirt
cilinder (Hungarian) top hat
gulp (Dutch) fly (in trousers)

Hairdressed to kill

And hair is one very obvious place for the drastic makeover:

rikuruto-katto (Japanese) a short haircut supposed to
impress prospective employers (literally, recruit cut)

wu-masweeswe (Kalanga, Botswana) shaving the hair in a
sinuous outline across the forehead

emperifollado(a) (Latin American Spanish) dressed to kill,
particularly when it involves a complicated hairdo

Topfschnitt (German) a certain haircut that looks a bit as if
the hairdresser put a saucepan on someone's head and cut
all around it (literally, saucepan cut)

Frigate

Make sure not to overdo it:

cerone (Italian) excessive make-up applied on one's face
(literally, grease paint)

itoyewaton (Dakota, USA) to wear anything that makes one
look frightful

age-otori (Japanese) formally styling one's hair for a coming-
of-age ceremony, but looking worse than before

Verschlimmerung (German) an improvement for the worse

die Fregatte (German) a heavily made-up old woman
(literally, frigate)

yubisakibijin (Japanese) a woman who spends a lot of her
salary tending to her fingernails

Ugly beautiful

Though there are hundreds of poetic English words for different beautiful colours, there are very few for those at the less
pleasant end of the spectrum. The Ojibway of North America
say **osawegisan**, which means making something yellow with
smoke, nicotine-stained. The Pali of India have a word for the
bluish-black colour of a corpse – **vinilaka** – which literally
means resembling neither father nor mother. The Amerindian
Mingo words for the basic colours are just as evocative:

uiskwanyë'ta'ê' the colour of rotten wood (brown)
unöwö'ta'ê' the colour of limestone or plaster (white)
uyë'kwææ'ê' the colour of smoke (grey)
tsitkwææ'ê' the colour of bile (yellow)

Berlin backsides

Just because you can't see your own backside doesn't mean that others can't. The Germans certainly notice these things:

Arschgeweih a large symmetrical tattoo on the lower back, just above the bottom, resembling the shape of antlers
Liebestoeter unattractive underwear (literally, love killer)
Maurerdekoltee a bricklayer's cleavage (the part of a man's backside you can see when he stoops deeply and his trouser waistband goes down a little bit)

Sails set

All over the world, people enjoy escaping from their intractable shape in a fine outfit:

kambabalegkasan (Maguindanaon, Philippines) the act of wearing new clothes
sich auftakeln (German) to get all dolled up (literally, with all sails set)
housunprässit (Finnish) trouser creases
fifi (Argentinian Spanish) a fashion-conscious man, dandy
kopezya (Mambwe, Zambia) tipping his hat down over his eyes
pagalong (Maranao, Philippines) to look at oneself in the mirror

Kangaroo teeth

Though what works in one place won't necessarily work in another:

nastā (Hindi) a hole bored in the septum of the nose
wo-kûs'-i-ûk (Maliseet, Canada) a necklace of claws
kechchai (Tamil) little tinkling bells tied to the legs
wowoodteyadla (Kaurna Warra, Australia) two or four kangaroo teeth bound together with hair and covered with grease and red ochre, worn on the forehead by fully initiated men
okpukpu (Igbo, Nigeria) an ivory bangle worn by women with ten or more children, and sometimes by men to demonstrate their proven expertise
borsello (Italian) a man's handbag

Hand-me-downs

'Those who have fine clothes in their chests can wear rags,' say the Italians, but in other parts of the world it's not always true that the higher up you are in society the more likely you are to dress down:

s chuzhovo plecha (Russian) second-hand clothes (literally, from a stranger's shoulder)
kamaeieia (Gilbertese, Oceania) to wear a garment until it is in tatters
xúng xính (Vietnamese) to be dressed in oversized clothes
mabelebele (Setswana, Botswana) the rags and tatters worn by a madman, a pauper or a traditional doctor

Designer knitwear

The two extremes of women's intense relationship with clothes are chronicled by the Japanese. At one end there is **nitto-onna**, a woman so dedicated to her career that she has no time to iron blouses and so resorts to dressing only in knitted tops; and at the other there are **ippaiyoku**, women whose every garment and accessory are made by the same designer.

Fashionista

Most try to keep up with what everyone else is wearing, but there will always be some, thankfully, who remain gloriously independent:

cowichan (British Columbia, Canada) a vividly patterned sweater

buddi (Tamil) someone who wears thick glasses

lambung (Maguindanaon, Philippines) to wear very big clothes

agadagba (Igbo, Nigeria) men's underpants woven from a mix of cotton, grass and tree bark

arse gras (Tok Pisin, Papua New Guinea) a bunch of tanket leaves stuck into a belt to cover a man's backside

So village

For as long as clothes have been around, people have sneered or laughed at what others have chosen to wear:

topeewalla (Hindi) one who wears a hat, generally a European

kampungan (Indonesian) someone who is incredibly out of fashion, outdated (literally, so village)

hemdsärmelig (German) someone who behaves very rustically (literally, shirt-sleeved)

ta-oiny (Car, Nicobar Islands) clothes-wearing foreigners

samopal (Russian) home-made clothing sold under commercial labels (literally, a home-made cap gun)

Clodhoppers

Though hopefully not what they put on their feet:

gállot (Sami, North Scandinavia) a shoe made out of hide
taken from the head of a reindeer

fittocks (Scots) the feet of stockings cut off and worn as shoes

kirza (Russian) imitation leather boots

innesko (Swedish) an indoor shoe

jorg (Scots) the noise of shoes when full of water

Barely there

But then again isn't one of the most enjoyable things about dressing up coming home and stripping off?

huhu (Rapanui, Easter Island) to take off one's clothes in one
go, with a pull

byambula (Tsonga, South Africa) to walk in the open completely naked

Just make sure that when you get dressed again there's no confusion …

vrenge (Norwegian) the action of putting right clothes which
are inside out

lopodutes (Ancient Greek) one who slips into another's
clothes

terchausser (Gallo, France) to put the right foot into the left
boot and vice versa

embasan (Maguindanaon, Philippines) to wear clothes while
taking a bath

Don't judge a book by its cover

ngam tae rup, jub mai horm (Thai) great looks but bad
  breath

l'abito non fa il monaco (Italian) clothes do not make the
  monk

quem vê caras não vê corações (Portuguese) he who sees
  face doesn't see heart

odijelo ne čini čovjeka (Croatian) a suit doesn't make a man

het zijn niet alleen koks die lange messen dragen
  (Dutch) it's not only cooks who carry long knives

II.
Stretching Your Legs

zemheride yoğurt isteyen, cebinde bir inek taşır (*Turkish*)
he who wants yoghurt in winter must carry a cow in his pocket

Travel broadens the mind, they say. But in these days of mass tourism and carbon footprints there's a lot to be said for staying exactly where you are:

dlanyaa (Tsonga, South Africa) to lie on one's back with one's legs apart, gorged with food

lezarder (French) to lie around basking in the sun like a lizard

bafalala (Tsonga, South Africa) to lie face down in the sun, to lie asprawl in the open

naptakhpaya (Dakota, USA) to lie on one's belly and rest on one's arms

ngumulo (Tagalog, Philippines) to put both hands under the head when lying down

kagwia (Yamana, Chile) to go upstairs and lie down

Presiding

Not that you have to remain entirely supine to relax:

sumernichat (Russian) to sit outside in the evening doing nothing

seranggong (Malay) to sit with one's elbows on the table

kem-lo-re (Car, Nicobar Islands) to sit on someone's knee

upa-nishád (Sanskrit) sitting down at the feet of another to listen to his words

mâhove'êsee'e (Cheyenne, USA) to have a tired bottom from sitting

babaran-on (Ik, Nilo-Saharan) to sit in a group of people warming up in the early morning sun

⁓ Go to hell

'See Naples and die' we're all told, but what do you do after you've visited these admirably named places?

Ecce Homo, Switzerland

Egg, Austria

Hell, Norway

No Guts Captain, Pitcairn Island

Saddam Hussein, Sri Lanka

Sexmoan, Philippines

Silly, Belgium

Starbuck Island, Polynesia

Wedding, Germany

Enviable

The Yamana people of Chile have clearly had plenty of time to think about the many permutations of sitting: **utapanus-mutu** is to sit by the side of a person but not close to him; **usata-ponur mutu** is to turn round and sit facing someone; **mumbu-moni** is to sit holding anything between one's lips; while **kupas-aiiua-mutu** is to sit envying a person.

Upright

If you get to your feet it doesn't necessarily mean that you're on the move:

pratyutthān (Hindi) rising from a seat as a mark of respect
hó'kôhtôheóó'e (Cheyenne, USA) to stand leaning on a cane
suka-a.-moni (Yamana, Chile) to stand dreaming
hangama (Tsonga, South Africa) to stand with one's feet wide apart (like a man taking up all the space before a fire)
távoeóó'e (Cheyenne, USA) to stand looking goofy

Pedestrian

But once you've put one foot in front of the other there's really no going back:

semeioton (Greek) walking on the spot

diváviharana (Sinhala, Sri Lanka) walking about in the day time

hanyauka (Rukwangali, Namibia) to walk on tiptoe on warm sand

ha shtatin (Albanian) to walk backwards in a bowed position

Tip-tip-toe

Although this simple action comes in many different styles:

vukurukuru (Tsonga, South Africa) the noisy walk of a person in a bad temper

endal (Malay) to walk with the head and shoulders held back and the breast and stomach thrust forward

bikrang (Bikol, Philippines) to walk with the legs apart as if there was some injury to the area of the crotch

onya (Setswana, Botswana) to walk at a slow pace nodding one's head

lonjak (Malay) to walk affectedly on tiptoe

vydelyvat krendelya (Russian) to stagger, to walk crookedly (literally, to do the pretzel)

uluka (Mambwe, Zambia) a person who walks as if he were carried by the wind

The trees are blazed

Be sure you know where you're going...

> **gembelengan** (Indonesian) moving around without any certain direction
>
> **sakgasakgile** (Setswana, Botswana) to wander about like a homeless orphan

... that the way ahead is clear:

> **jimbulwila** (Luvale, Zambia) to walk in an unknown place, where there is no clear path
>
> **tlhotlhomela** (Tsonga, South Africa) to wriggle one's way through thick bush

... that you've decided whether to cover your tracks:

> **kodhola** (Oshindonga, Namibia) to leave marks in the sand when walking
>
> **kikinawadakwaidade** (Ojibway, North America) marks on the trees for the traveller to find the trail through the wood (literally, the trees are blazed)
>
> **tuuna-gamata** (Yamana, Chile) to walk over where others have walked before and thus make the tracks indistinct

… and that the conditions are suitable:

hanmani (Dakota, USA) to walk in the night
tidiwitidiwi (Kerewe, Tanzania) dragging one's steps through
    sand or mud
pfumbura (Shona, Zimbabwe) to walk raising dust
splerg (Scots) to walk splashing in mud
shatoka (Lozi, Niger-Congo) to jump from one stone or log to
    another

False friends

lost (Cornish) tail, queue
halt (Swedish) lame, limping
loop (Dutch) walk, gait
murmur (Persian) to creep
silk (Bashgali, India) to be slippery

That sinking feeling

As what could be worse than losing your footing ...

anamni (Dakota, USA) to give way under the foot (as snow does, when there is water under it)

bawela (Tsonga, South Africa) to sink away in deep mud

kawan (Manobo, Philippines) to walk on air above the ground (for example, when walking in the dark and groping for footing, to step and not find footing where you expected it)

... mistaking the ground:

péese'ov (Cheyenne, USA) to step on someone's fingers

trapu psa (Sranan Tongo, Surinam) to step on someone's feet in passing

gobray (Boro, India) to fall into a well unknowingly

... or otherwise getting into difficulties:

dungkal (Bikol, Philippines) to trip and fall head first

gadngád (Tagalog, Philippines) falling on one's nose

kaiyotan (Dakota, USA) to fall in attempting to sit down

ra (Tsonga, South Africa) to fall backwards on something hard

platzen (German) to fall over and burst

af-vegar (Old Icelandic) fallen on one's back and unable to rise

pipilili (Tsonga, South Africa) to fall and roll a few times before stopping

Beard in the postbox

Oh dear, you're back where you started:

nu sitter du med skagget i brevladan (Swedish) now you are stuck (literally, now you are sitting with your beard in the postbox)

IDIOMS OF THE WORLD

To carry coals to Newcastle

Eulen nach Athen tragen (German) taking owls to Athens

yezdit' b Tulu s svoim samovarom (Russian) he's going to Tula, taking his own samovar

vendere ghiaccio agli eschimesi (Italian) selling ice to the Eskimos

echar agua al mar (Spanish) to throw water into the sea

es como llevar naranjas a Valencia (Spanish) it is like taking oranges to Valencia

vizet hord a Dunába (Hungarian) he is taking water to the Danube

gi bakerbarn brød (Norwegian) to give bread to the child of a baker

vender mel ao colmeeiro (Portuguese) to sell honey to a beemaster

12.
Upping Sticks

suusan tsetsnees yavsan teneg deer
(*Mongolian*)
*a travelling fool is better than a sitting wise
person*

You can't spend your whole life flopping around in one place. Sooner or later, whatever traveller's nerves you may feel, you just have to up sticks and go:

gabkhron (Boro, India) to be afraid of witnessing an adventure

resfeber (Swedish) to be jittery before a journey

andlamuka (Tsonga, South Africa) to pack up and depart, especially with all one's belongings, or to go for good

bishu (Chinese) to be away from a hot place in the summer

campanilismo (Italian) local pride, attachment to the vicinity (literally, bell tower-ism – referring to the fact that people do not want to travel so far as to be out of sight of the bell tower)

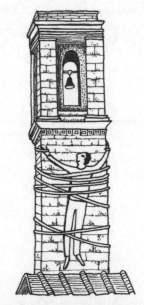

Reindeer's piss

A journey's a journey whether you are going near …

poronkusema (Finnish) the distance equal to how far a reindeer can travel without a comfort break – about 5 kilometres (literally, reindeer's piss)

tonbogaeri (Japanese) to go somewhere for business and come right back without staying the night (literally, dragonfly's return)

… or far:

donde San Pedro perdió el guarache (Mexican Spanish) to the back of beyond; at the ends of the earth (literally, where St Peter lost his sandal)

tuwatauihaiw-ana (Yamana, Chile) to be absent a very long time and thus cease to remember or care for your country and people (as an emigrant might after a long absence)

False friends

travel (Norwegian) busy
crush (Romani) to get out
bias (Malay) deflected from its course
grind (Dutch) gravel

Wanderlust

Some people just can't wait to get going:

Tapetenwechsel (German) being bored with the place you're
in and wishing to go somewhere else (literally, let's change
the wallpaper)

echarse el pollo (Chilean Spanish) to get out of town (literally, to throw out the chicken)

amenonéhne (Cheyenne, USA) to sing while walking along

henkyoryugaku (Japanese) young women who in their
twenties and thirties rebel against social norms and travel
abroad to devote time to an eccentric art form such as
Balinese dancing (literally, studying abroad in the wild)

Tag-along

But it can get lonely out there, so consider taking a companion:

uatomoceata (Yamana, Chile) to pass your arm within another's and bring him along, as friends do

adi (Swahili) to accompany a person part of their way out of
politeness

Lebensgefahrte (German) one who travels life's road with
you

nochschlepper (Yiddish) a fellow traveller, tag-along, camp
follower, pain in the arse (literally, someone who drags
along after someone else)

ku-sebeya (Ganda, Uganda) to travel with one's husband

Wire donkey

Travel on two wheels is always economical, and can be more or less environmentally sound:

der Drahtesel (German) a bicycle (literally, wire donkey)

washa (Luvale, Zambia) a bicycle (from the sound it makes as it runs along a narrow path brushing against bushes)

stegre (Sranan Tongo, Surinam) to ride a bicycle or a motorized two-wheel vehicle on only the back wheel

bromponie (Afrikaans) a motor scooter (literally, a growling or muttering pony)

Loosely bolted

And though four wheels are faster, there is many a pitfall:

sakapusu (Sranan Tongo, Surinam) an unreliable vehicle, so called because you always need to get out (**saka**) and push (**pusu**)

galungkung (Maguindanaon, Philippines) the rattling sound produced by a loosely bolted car

der Frischfleischwagen (German) an ambulance (literally, fresh meat delivery van)

parte (Chilean Spanish) a traffic ticket; also a baptism or wedding invitation

gagjom (Tibetan) to set up a roadblock and then rob someone

Highway code

Sometimes the greatest danger on the road comes from other users:

faire une queue de poisson (French) to overtake and cut in close in front of a car (literally, to do a fishtail)

Notbremse ziehen (German) to swerve away at the last moment (literally, to pull the handbrake)

shnourkovat' sya (Russian) to change lanes frequently and unreasonably when driving (literally, to lace boots)

autogangsteri (Finnish) a hit-and-run driver

Lucky number plates

The Chinese particularly like car number plates with 118, which is pronounced **yat yat fatt** in Cantonese and sounds like 'everyday prospers'; 1128 sounds like 'everyday easily prospers'; and 888 'prosper, prosper, prosper'. A number plate with 1164 is not popular because it sounds like **yat yat look say**, which can mean 'everyday roll over and die'.

A Hong Kong owner (i.e. a Cantonese speaker) would favour a number plate with just 32168, which sounds like **sang yee yat low fatt**, meaning 'a very profitable business all the way'.

Japanese cars can't have the licence plate 4219 because that could be read as **shi ni i ku**, which means something along the lines of 'going to death'.

Jesus's magimix

If all else fails there's always public transport (with all the delights that that entails). As the Germans say, 'We are all equal in the eyes of God and bus drivers':

gondola (Chilean Spanish) a municipal bus
Lumpensammler (German) the last train (literally, rag collector)
Luftkissenboot (German) a hovercraft (literally, air-cushion vehicle)

Or perhaps it's time to splash out on something special:

magimiks belong Yesus (Tok Pisin, Papua New Guinea) a helicopter

Pushmepullyou

Japanese subways are so crowded that they employ special packers to push people on and others to untangle them and get them off when they get to a station. The pushers-on are addressed as **oshiya-san** (honourable pusher) and the pullers-off as **hagitoriya-san** (honourable puller).

Unknown and uneasy

The truth is that travel is rarely as glamorous as it's portrayed. So whatever happens, keep your nerve:

far-lami (Old Icelandic) unable to go further on a journey
kalangkalang (Manobo, Philippines) to be overtaken by
    night on a journey with no place to stay and nothing to eat
asusu (Boro, India) to feel unknown and uneasy in a new
    place
bu fu shultu (Chinese) not accustomed to the climate or food
    of a new place (said of a stranger)
wewibendam (Ojibway, North America) being in a hurry to
    return home

Empty trip

And sometimes you will be surprised by unexpected rewards:

inchokkilissa (Alabama, USA) to be alone and experience the
    quietness of a location
uluphá (Telugu, India) supplies given to any great personage
    on a journey, and furnished gratis by those who reside on
    the route

Even if you never actually go:

kara-shutcho (Japanese) to pay or receive travel expenses for
    a trip not actually taken (literally, empty business trip)

Travellers' tales

Always remember that, as the French say, '**À beau mentir qui vient de loin**', travellers from afar can lie with impunity:

iwaktehda (Dakota, USA) to go home in triumph having taken scalps

To beat about the bush

y aller par quatre chemins (French) to get there by four paths

iddur mal-lewża (Maltese) to go round the almond

å gå som katten rundt den varma grøten (Norwegian) to walk like a cat around hot porridge

menare il can per l'aia (Italian) to lead the dog around the yard

emborrachar la perdiz (Spanish) to get the partridge drunk

13.
Home Sweet Home

Padres, primos e pombos. Os dois primeiros, não servem para casar. Os dois últimos só servem para sujar a casa (*Portuguese*)
Priests, cousins and pigeons. The first two are not good to marry. The last two only make the house dirty

Location, location, location

'Choose the neighbour before the house' goes an old Syrian proverb; and it's as well to check out the people living nearby before you move in:

kwarts-idioot (Dutch) next door to an idiot
espreitadeira (Portuguese) a woman who spies on her neighbours
geitonopoulo/a (Greek) the boy/girl next door
buurvrouw (Dutch) a neighbour's wife
búa-grettur (Old Icelandic) a quarrel between neighbours
keba (Myanmar) a village reserved for outcasts and beggars

Nesting

If you have space and time, and hopefully some good materials, your best bet is probably to build your own:

u'skwææi (Mingo, USA) a brick (literally, cooked stone)
skvorets (Russian) a person transporting building materials to a dacha in a car (literally, a starling – with reference to nest building)
méygirathu (Tamil) to cover a house with grass, leaves, etc.
maaia (Yamana, Chile) to build wigwams here and there, as a large number of people flocking to a place will do rather than crowd into two or three existing wigwams

Pulling together

Things always work out better if you've got people to help you:

akittittuq (Iñupiat, Inuit) a stitch used for sewing a tent made by having one person on the inside while the other is outside (the one on the inside pushes the needle out so that the other person can pull the thread through; the person on the outside then pushes the needle in for the other person to pull); the same stitch is used for sewing a window into place

dugnad (Norwegian) working together in everyone's interest without getting paid (for example, moving into a house, painting, building a cabin, etc.; also applies to parents coming together to paint a kindergarden, or everyone in an apartment building cleaning inside and outside the house together)

imece (Turkish) a social gathering at which everyone pitches in to help a neighbour undertake a large task

False friends

abort (German) lavatory
bang (Korean) room
dig (Gaelic) ditch
sir (Arabic) crack of the door
street (Norwegian) gate
rub (Croatian) edge

Flagging the beam

In Surinam, when the main roof beam of a new house is in place they have a celebration they call **opo-oso**, at which a flower or flag is nailed to the end of the beam, some beer is sprayed on the front of the building and then the builders, owner and others have a drink to celebrate.

Dutch decor

The Dutch have two useful expressions: **kneuterig** describes a particularly bourgeois type of stinginess which someone might display if they spent a fortune buying a new house and then furnished it with the cheapest fittings available, all in the name of saving money; and its opposite **een vlag op een modderschuit**, excessive decoration of a common thing, or trying to make the ugly beautiful (literally, a flag on a mud barge).

Chinese whispers

It is an increasingly common practice to transliterate foreign proper nouns into Chinese characters that sound similar to the original word but give the Western name a highly positive connotation to Chinese ears:

adian	Athens	proper law
zhili	Chile	wisdom benefit
deli	Delhi	virtue hometown
faguo	France	method country
henghe	Ganges	everlasting river
haiya	The Hague	sea tooth
ingguo	England	country of heroes
lundun	London	matching honest
meiguo	America	beautiful country
niuyue	New York	bond agreement
taiguo	Thailand	peaceful country

Frog in a well

The Germans have the wonderful word **Gemütlichkeit** for that particular quality of cosiness you can only ever feel at home. In that always-descriptive language, someone who prefers to stay at home is a **Stubenhocker**, literally, a room sitter; and in the end, however splendid the house, it's our intimate individual eyries we actually spend our time in:

> **pung** (Iban, Sarawak and Brunei) to keep to one's room
> **sucilwa** (Mambwe, Zambia) a man who never leaves his hut (literally, all smoked up)
> **kúpa-mandúka** (Sinhala, Sri Lanka) one who never leaves his home, one ignorant of the world (literally, a frog in a well)

The emperor's throne

Different cultures have very different approaches to what we euphemistically call the smallest room in the house. The Spanish have **excusado**, with its polite suggestion of excusing yourself, whereas the German term **wo sogar der Kaiser von China allein hingeht** literally means 'where the emperor of China goes by himself'. Once there, though, we all go through the same motions:

> **engkilu'** (Iban, Sarawak and Brunei) sticks or leaves used as toilet paper
> **zasedat'** (Russian) to sit on the toilet for a long time (literally, to preside)

Toilet museum

Some insist on trying to make us forget why we're there at all:

toirebijutsukan (Japanese) a trend whereby young women
moving into an apartment alone for the first time will go
to extreme lengths to decorate their lavatory, scent it with
perfume and stock it with interesting literature (literally,
toilet museum)

Spatially aware

We all know these domestic places and spaces; but not all languages have such precise words for them:

bakatoo (Mandinka, West Africa) the space between the bed and the wall

izungu (Mambwe, Zambia) the space between the bed and the ground

caukā (Hindi) a clean corner in the kitchen for having meals; a rectangular slab of stone

Giftschrank (German) a cupboard where things are kept that may only be lent out to someone with special permission (literally, poison cabinet)

antardvār (Hindi) a private door inside a house

rincón (Spanish) the internal corner (the external corner is **esquina**)

Besucherritze (German) the gap where the middle of three people lies when two single beds are pushed together (literally, a visitor's trench)

Crumb thief

The same is true of the clutter we fill our rooms up with; until, as the Russians say, '**Igolku nygde votknut**', there's nowhere you can throw a needle:

dur dicki mengri (Romani) a telescope (literally, far-seeing-thing)

hap laplap bilong wasim plet (Tok Pisin, Papua New Guinea) a dish cloth

kruimeldief (Dutch) a hoover (literally, a crumb thief)

Staubsauger (German) a vacuum cleaner (literally, dustsucker)

yötwënukwastahkwa' (Mingo, USA) radio (literally, people use it for spreading their voice out)

dinnilos dikkamuktar (Romani) television (literally, fool's looking box)

Flimmerkasten (German) television (literally, flickering box)

Whatever our circumstances, in the end, perhaps, we should just be grateful that we are **á-panna-griha** (Sanskrit), someone whose house has not fallen in.

To make a mountain out of a molehill

tehdä kärpäsestä härkänen (Finnish) to make a bull out of
a fly

se noyer dans un verre d'eau (French) to drown oneself in a
glass of water

til ka taad banaana or **rai ka pahaad banana** (Hindi) to
turn a sesame seed into a large tree or to turn a mustard
seed into a mountain

arcem e cloaca facere (Latin) to make a stronghold out of a
sewer

narediti iz muhe slona (Slovenian) to make an elephant
from a fly

14.
Dinner Time

kopeklerin duası kabul olsa gökten
kemik yağardı (*Turkish*)
*if dogs' prayers were accepted it would rain
bones from the sky*

Rushed breakfast

When it comes to eating there is, of course, no such thing as a typical meal:

munkavacsora (Hungarian) a working dinner

kamatuao (Gilbertese, Oceania) a meal for one who wakes during the night

bulunenekinoo (Mandinka, West Africa) the first meal cooked by a bride

ottobrata (Italian) a country outing or picnic in October

hwyaden (Welsh) the small amount of breakfast a newly married man has time to eat when leaving home for work after intimacy with his new wife (literally, a duck)

My tapeworm is talking

And there are still many parts of the world where you can't take any kind of refreshment for granted:

kemarok (Malay) ravenously hungry after an illness

hiukaista (Finnish) to feel hungry for something salty

paragadupu (Telugu, India) the state of the stomach before a person has broken his fast

fulumizya (Mambwe, Zambia) to cook quickly for somebody who is very hungry

étaomêhótsenôhtóvenestse napâhpóneehéhame (Cheyenne, USA) being very hungry (literally, my tapeworm can almost talk by itself)

Sampling

Particular skills are often required to make sure you've got the very best of the ingredients available:

kupit' arbuz navyrez (Russian) to buy a watermelon with the right to sample a section

pale (Scots) to test a cheese by an incision

athukkugirathu (Tamil) to press a fruit softly with the fingers

Stirring it up

And then time must be taken to get things correctly and thoroughly prepared:

jiigl (Buli, Ghana) to stir with much energy, to prepare a hard food that cannot be stirred with one hand

ri-noo-ko che-he-kuo (Car, Nicobar Islands) chopping up with spoons and forks

tikudeni (Maguindanaon, Philippines) to put the correct amount of rice into a pot to be cooked

loyly (Finnish) the wave of heat that engulfs you when you throw water on the hot stove

Surprise water

Now is the moment when a cook's individual skills can make all the difference to the end result. As the Chinese wisely say, 'Never eat in a restaurant where the chef is thin':

tliwat (Tagalog, Philippines) to pour a liquid several times between containers to mix or cool it well

bikkuri mizu (Japanese) a small amount of cold water added to a boiling pot of spaghetti or other noodles just before they are cooked (literally, surprise water: i.e. the cold water surprises the noodles)

ilas-ana (Yamana, Chile) to cut and spread meat open so that it cooks quicker

tuyong (Tagalog, Philippines) water added to make up for water lost (in cooking)

Dead dog

'Hunger is the best cook,' say the Germans, and it's true that when you're starving even the lightest snack will taste as good as anything you've ever eaten:

smörgås (Swedish) a sandwich (literally, butter goose)

ekiben (Japanese) a packed lunch dispensed from station kiosks

dokhlaya sobaka (Russian) a low-quality frankfurter (literally, a dead dog)

Xoox

For the fuller meal, what fine and varied ingredients the world offers:

jordgubbe (Swedish) a strawberry (literally, earth man)
ah (Arabic) egg white
xoox (Eastern Arabic) plums
sneisar-hald (Old Icelandic) the part of a sausage in which the pin is stuck
tsé-péene éškôseeséhotamého'évohkôtse (Cheyenne, USA) a pork sausage

Slug in the hole

Some ingredients might not be to everyone's taste:

lelita' (Iban, Sarawak and Brunei) an edible slug of the swampland
nido (Tagalog, Philippines) an edible bird's nest
brarah (Hebrew) second-rate fruits (specifically oranges)
kavavangaheti (Tsonga, South Africa) a dead animal so large that people cannot finish its meat (for example, hippo, whale or elephant)
cilh-vans (Hindi) the flesh of a kite (the eating of which is said to produce madness)
mmbwe (Venda, South Africa) a round pebble taken from a crocodile's stomach and swallowed by a chief

Cabbage or cheese

The Italians even approve or disapprove in terms of food:

come i cavoli a merenda totally out of place, inappropriate
(literally, like cabbage for a snack)
come il cacio sui maccheroni perfect (literally, like cheese
on pasta)

Your legs are long

The actual nosh itself is only part of it. Company is equally important, and in many parts of the world you simply have no idea who's
going to show up:

pakiroki (Rapanui, Easter Island) a pauper who comes to
someone else's house hoping to be invited to eat
jiao chang (Chinese) your legs are long (said of someone who
arrives just as something delicious is being served)
a la suerte de la olla (Chilean Spanish) to arrive at someone's house not knowing what food they will be offering
(literally, to the luck of the pot)
bufeťák (Czech) a guy who hangs around cafeterias and eats
leftovers
xenodaites (Ancient Greek) a devourer of guests or strangers

Say cheese

When trying to catch a person's attention and have him/her look into the lens, the old Czech photographers' phrase was **pozor, vyleti ptacek**, which literally means 'watch out, a bird will be released/fly out' (from the camera). In Serbia, people are asked to say **ptica**, 'bird'. Danish photographers have a variety of phrases they can use, but their favourite is **sig appelsin**, 'say orange'.

The English word cheese is often used because pronouncing it shapes the mouth into a smile. Other languages have adopted this method, with different words that have a similar sound or effect:

kimchi (Korean) a traditional fermented dish made of seasoned vegetables
qiezi (Mandarin) aubergine
cerise (French) cherry
whisky (Argentinian Spanish)

In Malta, people sometimes jokingly say **ġobon**, their word for cheese, which will obviously result in the exact opposite facial expression.

Gobbling it down

Sometimes your guests are so busy filling their faces that they forget about the politer aspects of sharing a meal:

fresser (Yiddish) someone who eats quickly and noisily

physiggoomai (Ancient Greek) to be excited by eating garlic

qarun (Persian) someone who eats two dates or two mouthfuls at once

bwakia (Swahili) to throw into the mouth (for example, pieces of food, nuts, tobacco)

komba (Chewa, South East Africa) to scrape a pot or dish with the forefinger, as children do

pelinti (Buli, Ghana) to move very hot food around inside one's mouth to avoid too close a contact

ikok (Ik, Nilo-Saharan) to knock bones together in order to take out and eat the marrow from inside

waphaka (South African Township) to eat faster than the rest

Miss Manners

Scoffing too fast can be just the start of the problem:

buttare giu tutto come un lavandino (Italian) to eat like a pig (literally, to throw down everything as if one were a sink)

muwel (Manobo, Philippines) to fill the mouth so that one cannot talk

hdaśna (Dakota, USA) to miss when putting food into one's mouth

xom-xoàm (Vietnamese) to speak while one's mouth is full

roic (Gaelic) the sumptuous feasting by boorish people without any of the refined manners of genteel society

False friends

sky (Swedish) gravy

tuna (Tuvaluan, Polynesia) prawn or eel

binlíd (Tagalog, Philippines) small broken particles of milled rice

dark (Albanian) evening meal

fig (Caribbean Creole) banana

Slow Food

So, instead, take your time and fully savour the experience:

fyompola (Mambwe, Zambia) to lick honey off the fingers
pisan zapra (Malay) the time needed to eat a banana

Menu envy

For some, the salad next door is always greener:

Futterneid (German) the desire to eat what is on another
person's plate (literally, feeding envy)
lyu mupusulo (Mambwe, Zambia) to eat so as to cheat
another out of his share of food
selongkar (Malay) to steal food off a plate
gagula (Tsonga, South Africa) to take food without permission, showing a lack of good manners

Picky

Others could do with feeling a bit hungry once in a while:

kieskauw (Dutch) a person who trifles with his food
malastigà (Tagalog, Philippines) being bored of eating the
  same food all the time
Krüsch (northern German) somebody who dislikes a lot of
  foods (and is therefore difficult to cook for)

My mouth is lonely

And some greedy pigs just don't know when to stop:

amuti (Rapanui, Easter Island) a glutton; someone who will
  eat anything, such as unripe or out-of-season fruit
akaska (Dakota, USA) to eat after one is full
ngang da (Vietnamese) to lose one's appetite because one has
  eaten between meals
kuchi ga samishii (Japanese) eating when you don't need to,
  for the sake of it or out of boredom (literally, my mouth is
  lonely)
knedlikový (Czech) rather partial to dumplings
hostigar (Chilean Spanish) to gorge on sweets to the point of
  nausea

Angel cake

In the end, though, it's all in the eye – or rather mouth – of the beholder. For better …

alsof er een engeltje op je tong piest (Dutch) utterly delicious, heavenly tasting (literally, as if an angel is urinating on your tongue)

kou fu (Chinese) the good luck prerequisite for having opportunities to eat delicious food (literally, mouth fortune)

… or worse:

panshey (Bengali) food that tastes rather flat

ichootakbachi (Alabama, USA) to leave a bad taste in the mouth

tomatoma (Mailu, Papua New Guinea) tasteless food

pikikiwepogosi (Ojibway, North America) having the taste of an animal that was tired out before it was killed

tsitlama (Setswana, Botswana) to make a wry face after eating or drinking something nasty

Restaurant review

Tired of cooking at home, not to mention doing the washing-up and putting-away, we may tell ourselves how nice it is to eat out. But though the fantasy is great, the reality is often less so:

Schlürfbude (German) a fast-food restaurant (literally, slurp dump)
dolorosa (Spanish) a restaurant bill (literally, painful)
Abendteuer (German) an expensive evening (literally, an adventure)

The condemned man is a final meal

Possibly the strangest takeaway of all is described by the Russian word **korova**: this is the unfortunate person that prison camp escapees take with them to eat over their period of flight and in their hideout (it literally means 'a cow').

Too many cooks spoil the broth

sendou ooku shite fune yama ni noboru (Japanese) too many captains and the boat will go up a mountain

qi shou, ba jiao (Chinese) seven hands, eight feet

idha kathira ar-rababina gharigat as-safina (Arabic) too many captains sink the ship

zo mangna go lhong mi tshu (Dzongkha, Bhutan) when there are too many carpenters the door cannot be erected

seul mui à vugulion a vez, e vez falloc'h gouarnet ar saout (Breton, France) the more cowherds there are, the worse the cows are looked after

puno baba, kilavo dijete (Croatian) with many midwives, the child will be lazy

veel varkens maken de spoeling dun (Dutch) many pigs make the slops sparse

zyada jogi math ujaad (Hindi) too many saints can ruin the monastery

troppi galli a cantar non fa mai giorno (Italian) with too many cocks singing it is never going to dawn

zuun yamaand jaran uhana (Mongolian) one hundred goats for sixty billy goats

u pyati nyanek dyetya byez glaza, u cemyorykh – byez golovy (Russian) when there are five nurses the child loses an eye – with seven nurses the child is finally found to lack a head

haber más capeadores que toros (Costa Rican Spanish) there are more bullfighters than bulls

15.
One for the Road

fra børn og fulde folk skal man høre
sandheden (*Danish*)
*from children and drunks you will hear the
truth*

The towel of a hippy

The quenching of thirst is another sensation that brings out evocative descriptions. In Chilean Spanish they say they are **tener mas sed que piojo de muneca**, thirstier than a louse on a doll; or again, in more contemporary usage, **to alla hippy**, than the towel of a hippy:

tarfa (Hausa, Nigeria) to pour out drop by drop
gargalacar (Portuguese) to drink from the bottle
funda (Swahili) to fill the mouth with water until the cheeks are distended
srann (Gaelic) a drink as deep as one's breath will permit
ngalela (Setswana, Botswana) to drink and drain the contents of a container in one go
avoir la dalle en pente (French) to have the throat on a slant (in order to be able to drink constantly)

The milky way

The men of the African Toubari and Massa tribes observe a rite called **gourouna** in which they retire for several months from ordinary pursuits and restraints and drink prodigious amounts of milk.

Social drinking

No one should **boire en Suisse** (French), drink alone in secret (literally, drinking in the Swiss way). It's always healthier to share the experience:

gonets (Russian) one sent to buy alcohol for friends (literally, a herald)

chistra (Breton, France) to go from farm to farm and ask for cider

cayetanas (Mexican Spanish) a code word for apple cider disguised in a beer bottle, ordered by cabaret hostesses who don't want to get drunk

afdrinken (Dutch) let's have a drink and be friends

glaoch (Irish) the act of calling for a round of drinks at a pub

Bob (Dutch) the designated driver, the one who sticks to one beer and drives everybody home from wherever they've been partying (Bob was the name used originally in a famous anti-drink-drive campaign)

Altered states

Soft drinks will satisfy our thirst, but are never as exciting as those which are a bit stronger. It's surely no coincidence that most of the best words about drinks and drinking involve alcohol. As the literal meaning of the Amerindian Mingo word for alcohol, **teka'niköëtényös**, has it, it changes minds from one way to another: whether it's beer you're drinking …

sampa (Rukwangali, Namibia) to taste beer with one's finger
bufferbiertje (Dutch) the beer that is standing next to the beer you're drinking and serves as a buffer in case you finish drinking your beer before you have a chance to get the barman's attention (literally, buffer beer)
der Diesel (German) a mixture of beer and cola

To your good health?

Around the world the commonest drinking toast is to good health: **Na zdravje** (Slovenian), **Salud** (Spanish), **Saúde** (Brazilian Portuguese), **Kia Ora** (Maori), **Egészségedre** (Hungarian), **Gezondheid** (Flemish). The Ukrainians take this to the next level with **Budmo!**, which means 'let us live forever!'

In contrast, the Scandinavian drinking toast **Skål!** (pronounced 'skoal') has a much more macabre background, as it originally meant 'skull'. The word is alleged to have come down from a custom practised by the warlike Vikings who used the dried-out skulls of their enemies as drinking mugs.

… or something rather more powerful:

Dreimännerwein (German) a wine so disgusting it takes three men to drink it (two men to make you drink it – you are the third)

kadamsana (Malawi) a very strong home-made spirit (literally, that which brings darkness during the day – aptly describing its knock-out effects)

Vodka vocabulary

The Russians, in particular, have a fine set of words for the many styles of tippling:

pogoda shepchet to take time off from work, or a desire to get drunk (literally, the weather is whispering)

busat' to drink alone

deryabnut' to drink quickly in order to warm up

gorlo to drink from the bottle

vspryskivat' to drink in celebration of a holiday or a new purchase (literally, to besprinkle)

daganyat' sya to drink in order to get drunk, to try to catch up with the amount of drinking that others have already done

otglyantsevat' to drink beer or wine after vodka (literally, to gloss a photo print)

ostogrammit'sya to drink 100 grams of vodka as a remedy for a hangover

False friends

full (Norwegian) drunk
grogi (Finnish) whisky and soda
pickle (Chilean Spanish) a person who drinks too much
jaw (Zarma, Nigeria) to be thirsty

On a slippery road

And all languages have evocative expressions for being drunk ...

sternhagelvoll (German) full of stars and hail
rangi-changi (Nepalese) slightly too multi-coloured
être rond comme une bille (French) to be as round as a
  marble
redlös (Swedish) ride free
andar cacheteando la banqueta (Mexican Spanish) to go
  along with one's cheek on the pavement

... and for the inevitable results of overdoing it:

khukhurhuteka (Tsonga, South Africa) to walk uncertainly,
  as a drunk man among people seated on the floor
midàbodàboka (Malagasy, Madagascar) to fall over frequently, as drunken men or people on a slippery road
mawibi (Ojibway, North America) drunken weeping
Backhendlfriedhof (Austrian German) a beer belly (literally,
  cemetery for fried chickens)
ne govori ou samoi muzh piatnisa (Russian) a shrug of
  understanding when sharing someone else's problems
  (literally, no need to explain, my husband is a drunk)

Under the monkey

For the French you are as sober as **un chameau** (a camel) but as drunk as **un cochon** (a pig), **une grive** (a thrush), or even **une soupe** (a soup). In Lithuanian you can also be drunk as a pig (**kiaulė**), or then again as a bee (**bitelė**) or a shoemaker (**šiaučius**). Elsewhere you can be **drvo pijan** (Macedonian) drunk as a tree; **jwei ru ni** (Mandarin) drunk as mud; **orracho como una uva** (Cuban Spanish) drunk as a grape; **bull som en kaja** (Swedish) drunk as a jackdaw; **itdek mast** (Uzbek) drunk as a dog; or **einen Affen sitzen haben** (German) to be dead drunk (literally, to have a monkey sit on one).

The morning after

It's only when you get home that you may start to wonder what on earth possessed you:

rhwe (Tsonga, South Africa) to sleep on the floor without a mat and usually drunk and naked

gidravlicheskiy budil'nik (Russian) a full bladder (literally, an hydraulic alarm clock)

sasamudilo (Ndebele, Southern Africa) a drink of beer in the morning after a debauch, a pick-me-up

peragar (Byelorussian) the residual taste of alcohol in the mouth

Vineyard flu

And all drinking cultures have inventive expressions for the horrors of the morning after:

avoir la gueule de bois (French) to have a wooden mouth

babalasi (Venda, South Africa) a trembling hangover

futsukayoi (Japanese) a hangover (literally, second day drunk)

winderdgriep (Afrikaans) a hangover (literally, vineyard flu)

einen Kater haben (German) to have a hangover (literally, to have a tomcat)

scimmia (Italian) to have a hangover (literally, a monkey)

IDIOMS OF THE WORLD

Don't cry over spilt milk

paid â chodi pais ar ôl piso (Welsh) don't lift a petticoat
after peeing

kusat sebe lokti (Russian) to bite one's elbows

nasi sudah menjadi bubur (Indonesian) the rice has
become porridge

eső után köpönyeg (Hungarian) coat after rain

16.
All in a Day's Work

yesli khochetsya rabotat' lyag pospi
i vsyo proydyot (*Russian*)
*if you feel an urge to work take a nap and it
will pass*

Pounce and decoy

Time was when going out to work meant leaving the cave or hut to forage for food:

mbwandira (Chichewa, Malawi) to catch a small animal like a bird or mouse by pouncing on top of it

puyugaktuq (Iñupiat, Inuit) to approach a sea mammal by crawling

tamigata (Yamana, Chile) to form together in a continuous line in order to drive birds up into a creek and then hemming them round to cut off their retreat to the open water

kanghanzila (Mambwe, Zambia) he who stands behind the game and imitates the lion's roar so as to drive the game into the nets

sendula (Mambwe, Zambia) to find accidentally a dead animal in the forest (and be excited at the thought that a lion or leopard could be still around)

walakatla (Tsonga, South Africa) to fling down in disgust, as a hunter does with his spears when returning empty-handed

Point blank

In our rapidly developing world, this is obviously less and less the case, as age-old skills are replaced by a more up-to-date weapon:

paltik (Kapampangan, Philippines) a home-made gun
otselask (Estonian) a point-blank shot
tsikinika (Oshindonga, Namibia) to shoot something at close
   range

Dodo

Even if the matching cunning of animals remains much the same:

debideboo (Mandinka, West Africa) a bird which pretends
   not to be able to fly but slips away any time an attempt is
   made to catch it
kavraq (Iñupiat, Inuit) a wounded caribou that runs away
   unobserved
ugutur-kona-ina (Yamana, Chile) to go about on the water
   evading sight; to hide as ducklings or goslings do to evade
   the hunter
vulwa-vulwa-vulwa (Tsonga, South Africa) to run a little, stop
   and look round before proceeding, like a buck anxious not
   to be seen

Spear hurling

Out on the seas and oceans, however, the traditional tools of hook and net have not been seriously superseded; nor have the associated skills:

zekumuna (Luvale, Zambia) to pull out a fish which flies off the hook and falls onto the ground

alatkaqtuq (Iñupiat, Inuit) to scan the landscape from an elevated point, to look into water for signs of fish

ukomona (Yamana, Chile) to hurl the spear at fish, but at no special one, hoping to spear one among the shoal

wasswa (Ojibway, North America) spearing fish at night by the light of a torch

Eel dribbling

In the countless islands of the Pacific, such techniques have been carefully honed:

kikamu (Hawaiian) the gathering of fish about a hook that they hesitate to bite

atua tapa (Rapanui, Easter Island) the orientation point for fishermen, which is not in front of the boat, but on the side

hakakau (Hawaiian) to stand with precarious footing, as on the edge of a canoe looking for squid

'ea'ea (Hawaiian) to cover the eyebrows, as a fisherman shading the eyes while looking into deep water for fish

ka ro'iro'i i te koreha (Rapanui, Easter Island) to dribble on the eel, to drop your spittle, mixed with chewed bait, into the water to attract the eel

Sea women

In Japan, abalone fishing is often done in husband and wife teams. The women, who are thought to be better at holding their breath and withstanding the cold for long periods, do the pearl diving, while the husbands take charge of the boat and the lifeline. The wives are known as **ama** – 'sea women'.

Bamboo cutters

Once the world moved on from hunting and gathering, a degree of occupational specialization was bound to creep in:

baradi'l (Arabic) a maker of donkey saddles

murd-shuy (Persian) a washer of dead bodies

ngmoruk-yaaroaba (Buli, Ghana) a ritual rain-maker

médara (Telugu, India) belonging to the caste that cut bamboos and live by selling them

gardziiba (Tibetan) an astrologist or a person in charge of the cups and dishes during parties

bakamyi (Rwanda and Burundi dialect) a person credited with supernatural powers who milked the royal cows

Mekametz (Talmudic Hebrew) a man who gathers dog faeces so that he may hand them over to the **Burskai**, men who process animal skins

Angel makers

As societies became more developed, so jobs became more rarified ...

netty (Scots) a woman who traverses the country in search of wool

sunba (Tibetan) someone who looks after irrigation canals

bagaceiro (Portuguese) a workman who feeds sugar-cane husks into a furnace

poppendokter (Dutch) a mender of dolls (literally, a doll doctor)

catadeira (Portuguese) a woman who culls coffee beans by hand

faiseur d'anges (French) an illegal abortionist (literally, an angel maker)

paçaci (Turkish) a man who sells sheep's trotters

khāndika (Sanskrit) a seller of sugar plums

bengaleiro (Portuguese) an umbrella maker or salesman

False friends

trafik (Hungarian) tobacconist
agenda (French) notebook, diary
basin (Turkish) the press
fabric (Russian) factory
pasta (Portuguese) briefcase, folder

Soul plumbers

… until we end up with occupations that are entirely sophisticated and modern:

amanuensis (Dutch) a laboratory attendant

arquitonto (Central American Spanish) a stupid architect

basura (Spanish) rubbish inspectors

dal'noboishitsa (Russian) a prostitute who specializes in a clientele of truckers

değnekçi (Turkish) an unofficial/self-appointed parking attendant

Seelenklempner (German) a psychiatrist (literally, a soul plumber)

culero (Spanish) a drug smuggler who hides the drugs in his rectum

jasusa (Arabic) a woman spy

profesores taximetros (Columbian Spanish) part-time professors who hold a number of teaching positions at various institutions from and to which they rush by taxi (literally, taxicab professors)

Hippopotomonstrosesquipedalianism (the practice of using long words)

The Germans are renowned for their love of long words where several words are compounded to form an extremely specific word, often to do with the world of work, such as:

Donaudampfschifffahrtsgesellschaftskapitänsjacken-knopfloch the buttonhole in the jacket of a captain of the Danube steam boat company

or **Reichseisenbahnhinundherschiebershäuschen** the little house of the state railway track shunter

But other languages also have their own lengthy words:

megszentségtelenithetetlenségeskedéseltekért (Hungarian) for your unprofaneable actions

kindercarnavalsoptochtvoorbereidingswerkzaamheden (Dutch) preparation activities for a children's carnival procession

inconstitucionalissimamente (Portuguese) very unconstitutionally

prijestolonaslijednikovica (Croatian) wife of an heir to the throne

Low profile

Of course, to do a job properly, certain key skills are useful:

aprovechar (Spanish) to get the best out of or make the most of an opportunity

diam ubi (Malay) to work quietly or with a low profile until successful

kamgar (Persian) one who accomplishes whatever he wishes

dub-skelper (Scots) one who goes his way regardless of mud and puddles (used light-heartedly of a young bank clerk whose duty it is to run about giving notice that bills are due)

coyote (Mexican Spanish) a person who handles certain troublesome legal procedures at government agencies on behalf of third parties and for a fee, by means of kick-backs and/or bribes (literally, coyote, a wolflike wild dog)

Horn diggers

However, we should never underestimate the virtue of good, old-fashioned graft:

greadan (Gaelic) spending a considerable time and giving all one's might to anything

balebosteven (Yiddish) to bustle like a meticulous housewife

ryt' rogom zemlyu (Russian) to make great efforts (literally, to dig up the ground with one's horn)

echar la casa por la ventana (Latin American Spanish) to go all out (literally, to throw the house out of the window)

sisu (Finnish) obstinate determination, heroic guts, stubborn persistence

dumog (Tagalog, Philippines) to be absorbed in the fulfilment of one's task

Mice milkers

Even so, diligence isn't everything. There are some poor workers who bust a gut but fail to please simply because they can't see the bigger picture. The French describe this as **chercher midi à quatorze**, literally, to look for midday at two o'clock in the afternoon. To the Dutch, a person who pays excessive attention to detail is a **mierenneuker** – literally, an ant fucker; or, more charitably, a **muggenzifter** (mosquito sifter) or a **punaisepoetser** (pin polisher). But all cultures are colourful in their criticism:

Erbsenzaehler (German) someone concerned with small things (literally, counter of peas)

pilkunnussija (Finnish) an extreme pedant (literally, comma fucker)

taburaka (Gilbertese, Oceania) one who exaggerates rules and regulations, a stickler for the letter of the law

Mäusemelker (German) someone who eagerly concentrates on the nitty-gritty rather than the wider overview (literally, someone who milks mice)

gladit' shnurki (Russian) to be over-solicitous, to do too much (literally, to iron someone's shoelaces)

Jobsworth

Other colleagues bring other problems:

Schnarchnase (German) someone who is slow in acting (literally, snoring nose)

pezezengdeng (Manobo, Philippines) to be spoken to but sit motionless and ignore their request

reke (Yoruba, Nigeria, Benin and Togo) to wait in expectation of another's mistake

kyag-kyag (Tibetan) throwing obstacles in the way of another's work, out of spite

švejkování (Czech) deviously undermining your boss or circumventing your supervisor's wishes while appearing angelically innocent and even rather simple (in the manner of the *Good Soldier Svejk*, the novel by Jaroslav Hasek)

suthi vuttiya (Tamil) the method used by call centre employees to avoid taking people's calls by changing their place on the list

Promises, promises

At least you can rely on the hopeless, spiteful and devious to be counterproductive. Worse are those who promise to help but never deliver, or who rush around frantically but never get anywhere:

kaengeng (Gilbertese, Oceania) to say 'yes yes' and do nothing about it

llamarada de petate (Nahuatl, Mexico) an undertaking started with great enthusiasm and suddenly dropped (**petate** is a woven reed mat used for sleeping)

hubyahubyeka (Tsonga, South Africa) to hurry here and there achieving nothing

ningas-kugon (Tagalog, Philippines) the sudden spurt of enthusiasm followed by a slowing down and an eventual slipping back into old habits

robota ne vovk, v lis ne vtiče (Ukrainian proverb) I can get back to doing that later (literally, work is not a wolf, it doesn't run into the woods)

nakinaki (Mandinka, West Africa) to go here and there pretending to be busy in order to avoid work

mikka bouzu (Japanese) a quitter (literally, three-day monk: a person who leaves the monkhood only three days after taking his vows)

Pedalling in yoghurt

The French, in particular, have a fine range of metaphors for not getting things done for one reason or another. **Brasser de l'air** is to give the impression of being busy (literally, to shuffle the air); **peigner la girafe** is to waste time in idle pursuits (literally, to comb the giraffe); **pedaler dans le yaourt** means to be getting nowhere fast (literally, to be pedalling in yoghurt); while **un coup d'épée dans l'eau** is a wasted effort (literally, a sword blow into water).

Counting the stars

One would almost prefer to work alongside those who model their lives on the Mexican Spanish expression **el trabajo embrutece**, work brutalizes …

poltrone (Italian) lazybones (literally, easy chairs)

shitat zvyozdy (Russian) to twiddle one's thumbs (literally, to count the stars)

jeta (Swahili) a lazy person who does not stir himself to get the things he wants, but asks others to fetch them, even though the things may be quite near to him

bulat (Maguindanaon, Philippines) to have a phobia of certain jobs

imilila (Mambwe, Zambia) to work half-heartedly, all the time thinking about leaving

The company tribe

... or are perhaps waiting in hope for those sought-after positions that will surely, eventually, come up:

enchufe (Spanish) a cushy job (literally, a plug or socket)
anichado (Portuguese) hidden away, as in a niche; well-placed
   in a good job
der Tintenpisser (German) a bureaucrat (literally, ink pisser)
tagapagpaganáp (Tagalog, Philippines) an executive
ntlhelavasati (Tsonga, South Africa) a place where one works
   that is not too distant from home
shayo-zoku (Japanese) employees living extravagantly on
   company money (literally, the company tribe)

Sell out

Although it's wise to remember that blind loyalty to the organization is much overrated:

ser líder charro (Mexican Spanish) to be a union leader who
   sells out to company management
wegloben (German) to laud away (i.e. if a superior wants to
   get rid of a co-worker he draws up an exaggerated testimo-
   nial to ensure that the unloved staffer leaves the company)
extraknack (Swedish) a job on the side
kutu-loncat (Indonesian) someone who constantly moves
   from job to job for better prospects or wages (literally,
   jumping bug)

Lilies of the field

Perhaps the luckiest are those who don't have to do anything at all:

goyang kaki (Malay) to shake one's leg; to live comfortably without having to work hard; to live off one's land or fortune or legacy

caer en blandito (Latin American Spanish) to have a situation turn out extremely well without much effort (literally, to fall on a soft surface)

péter dans la soie (French) to live the life of Riley (literally, to fart in silk)

I D I O M S   O F   T H E   W O R L D

Bad workman blames his tools

el mal escribano le echa la culpa a la pluma/el cojo le echa la culpa al empedrado (Spanish) the poor writer blames the pen/the limping man blames the pavement

złej baletnicy przeszkadza rąbek u spódnicy (Polish) a poor dancer will be disturbed even by the hem of her skirt

'araj al jamal min shiffatu (Arabic) the camel limped from its split lip

plokhomu tantsory (i) yaytsa meshayut (Russian) a poor dancer is impeded (even) by his own balls

---

17.
Game Theory

kush nuk di ç'është lodhja, ai nuk di ç'është çlodhja (*Albanian*)
who does not know tiredness, does not know how to relax

Celebrating Monday

However hard we work, it's important to take time off, even if we have to be clever about how we arrange it:

hacer San Lunes (Mexican Spanish) to take Monday off because the weekend was too exhausting (literally, to celebrate St Monday)

puente (Spanish) bridge; the Spanish have their bank holidays on a Tuesday so that Monday will, on most occasions, be treated as a bridge day (an extra day of holiday), ensuring a four-day weekend; there is also a **viaducto**, which is when holidays fall on a Tuesday and a Thursday, thus enabling someone to take the whole week off

Slow start

How wonderful to let slip the usual routines, take your time, take it easy:

faire la grasse matinée (French) to sleep in (literally, to make a fat morning)

pegar(sele) las sábanas a (alguien) (Latin American Spanish) to oversleep (literally, to have the sheets stick to you)

guzu guzu suru (Japanese) being slow when you have something you should be doing; a half-wakeful sleep, especially in the morning when you have sort of woken up but are still playing with your dreams

faire le tour du cadran (French) to sleep the day away (literally, to do the tour of the clock's face)

Idle time

Even when one has fully woken up there's no pressure to do anything:

cangkul angin (Malay) hoeing the air; putting one's feet up in the air or doing useless things

Although sometimes the lack of pressure can be pressurizing in itself:

Zeit totschlagen (German) somebody who has free time but doesn't know what to do, so does something senseless (literally, to beat time to death)

egkila-kila (Maguindanaon, Philippines) to act foolishly as a means to combat boredom

tsurumun (Japanese) a single woman who dreads being alone on national holidays and invents reasons to visit friends

False friends

black (Swedish) ink
brief (German) letter
fart (French) ski wax
gong (Balinese) orchestra
war-side (Somali) newspaper
urinator (Latin) diver
rust (Dutch) rest or tranquillity

Cucumber troop

There are all kinds of things one can do with time off. What about watching some football? Fans would surely agree that few players can be a **peleon** (Puerto Rican Spanish), one who plays like Pele, but the Germans have gathered an evocative vocabulary for the highs (and lows) of watching a match:

der Schlachtenbummler a football fan who travels to support his team at home and away (literally, battle stroller)

der Hexenkessel a football stadium of the opposing team, with the fans creating a heated atmosphere (literally, witch's cauldron)

kleinklein passing the ball from player to player without a plan (literally, small small)

Blutgratsche a nasty tackle

die Gurkentruppe a team that plays badly and unprofessionally, a disaster area, incompetent bunch of players (literally, cucumber troop)

Aggro

Or one could take up a heavier or more demanding sport:

bariga (Tagalog, Philippines) being thrown down in wrestling (literally, the bigger end of an egg)

atuila (Yamana, Chile) to press down on someone and make his legs give way so that he can be held down

munasat (Persian) taking hold of one another's forelocks when fighting

binti (Manobo, Philippines) a test of strength in which one man stands with his legs apart and his opponent runs from behind and kicks him in the calf of the leg with his shin in an attempt to knock him over; they then change places and continue until one is clearly defeated or gives up because of the pain

Ski-lane terror

Up in the mountains, it's fast, dangerous, but always fun:

Pistenschreck (German) a skier you have to watch out for
(literally, ski-lane terrorist)

tulee! (Finnish) look out! I'm skiing/sledging down towards
you at high speed! (literally, it's coming!)

ahterijarrut (Finnish) falling off your skis and using your tail-
end to stop (literally, arse-brakes)

Fackelabfahrt (German) a flaming-torchlight ski-run down
the side of a steep snowy mountain, undertaken at night by
around fifty skiers

The sound of your heart racing

Every language has onomatopoeic words, whose sound and rhythm vividly describe the sound or action they describe:

hara hara doki doki (Japanese) the feeling of your heart racing when you're scared or nervous

nyurrugu (Yidiny, Australia) the noise of talking heard a long way off when the words cannot be made out

vuhubya-hubya (Tsonga, South Africa) the flapping of pendulous breasts of a woman hurrying

krog-krog (Tibetan) a sound produced by grinding hard brittle objects together

empap (Malay) the sound of a flat object falling on a soft surface

mswatswa (Chichewa, Malawi) the sound of footsteps on dry grass

ndlangandzandlangandza (Tsonga, South Africa) the sound of drums during an exorcism ritual, beaten to cure a possessed person

geeuw (Dutch) a yawn

guntak (Malay) the rattle of pips in a dry fruit

gwarlingo (Welsh) the rushing sound a grandfather clock makes before striking the hour

phut (Vietnamese) the noise of string or rope that snaps

zhaghzhagh (Persian) the noise made by almonds or by other nuts shaken together in a bag

schwupp (German) quick as a flash (short for **schwuppdiwupp**)

szelescic (Polish) the sound when someone folds paper (pronounced scheleshchich)

Taking a dip

Down by the sea, river or lakeside, the activity on our day off is altogether gentler:

nchala-nchala-nchala (Tsonga, South Africa) to swim noiselessly and swiftly

zaplyvats (Byelorussian) to swim far out

maulep (Maguindanaon, Philippines) a diver who can stay underwater for a long time, holding his breath

kataobairi (Gilbertese, Oceania) to go under the surface of the water with only one's nostrils above

terkapai-kapai (Malay) nervously moving the arms about (said of a bad swimmer)

tankah (Hawaiian Pidgin) a surfboard that seats six

limilimi (Hawaiian) to be turned over and over in the surf

Dizzy dancing

In many parts of the world, though, resources dictate that they have to make their own fun:

akkharikā (Pali, India) a game recognizing syllables written in the air or on one's back

antyākshrī (Hindi) a poetic competition in which a contestant recites a couplet beginning with the last letter recited by the previous contestant and which is then carried on by rival teams

kapana (Setswana, Botswana) to catch each other with both hands when taking turns to fall from a height

sikki (Ilokano, Philippines) a game played by tossing pebbles aloft and catching as many of them as possible on the back of the hand

pitz/pokolpok (Mayan, Central America) a game in which the object is to put a rubber ball through a stone ring using only hips, knees and elbows

mmamadikwadikwane (Setswana, Botswana) a game in which a child spins round until dizzy; it's also the term for ballroom dancing

Taking part

The Tagalog language of the Philippines has some great words to describe how – literally speaking – to play the game:

salimpusà asking someone to participate in a game to appease him, although he is not necessarily wanted

perdegana an agreement in certain games whereby the loser wins

haplít the final burst of energy when trying to win a race

Suits and tricks

If you're **grebleyi na kon'kakh** (Russian) incompetent at sports (literally, to row on skates), perhaps it's wiser to seek alternative thrills:

aéstomêhasené (Cheyenne, USA) to play cards for nothing; that is, to play without betting anything

hila' (Manobo, Philippines) to take a trick with a winning card

orobairi (Gilbertese, Oceania) to hit the nose of the loser in cards

Kiebitz (German) an onlooker at a card game who interferes with unwanted advice

kofu kofu (Sranan Tongo, Surinam) a bet where the winner gets to hit the loser

Live entertainment

'Those who have free tickets to the theatre have the most criticism to make,' say the Chinese, but live entertainment can often be surprisingly enjoyable (for those taking part, that is):

recevoir son morceau de sucre (French) to be applauded the moment one first appears on stage (literally, to receive one's piece of sugar)

Sitzfleisch (German) the ability to sit through long and boring events without losing concentration (literally, seat meat)

One is fun

For the Japanese, gentler pleasures suffice:

sabi a feeling of quiet grandeur enjoyed in solitude (normally involving the beauty that comes from the natural ageing of things)

shibui a transcendently beautiful and balanced image, such as an autumn garden (literally, sour, astringent)

Stories with bears

Or one could indulge one's creative urges:

brat s potolka (Russian) to make something up (literally, to take something from the ceiling)

hohátôhta'hàne (Cheyenne, USA) to laugh while storytelling

istories gia arkudes (Greek) narrated events that are so wild and crazy it seems that they can't possibly be true (literally, stories with bears)

Bookmark

Or just kick back and enjoy the efforts of others:

kioskvältare (Swedish) a bestselling film/book (literally, something that tips over the booth)

hinmekuru (Japanese) to turn a page over violently

ádi (Telugu, India) a mark left in a book to show the place where the reader left off

Drooping tongue

However hard you try to prevent it, our day of recreation draws to its inevitable end:

bantil (Bikol, Philippines) to pinch the back of the neck to relieve weariness

traer la lengua de corbata (Latin American Spanish) to be worn out; to be exhausted (literally, to have your tongue hanging out like a man's tie)

Nodding off

And in different postures and places we drift into blessed oblivion:

corra-chodal (Gaelic) sleeping on one's elbow

clavar el pico (Latin American Spanish) to fall asleep in a sitting position

kakkawornendi (Kaurna Warra, Australia) to nod when sleeping

itanochi (Alabama, USA) to go to sleep on the floor or by a fire

yum (Car, Nicobar Islands) to sleep with someone in one's arms

Staying up

Among the Cheyenne people of the USA, sleep may be the last thing they get up to at night:

vóonâhá'ené to cook all night
vóonâhtóohe to howl all night
vóona'haso'he to ride a horse all night
vóonâše'še to drink all night
vóonêhasené to play cards all night
vóoneméohe to run all night
vóoneóó'e to stand all night
vóonévánéne to fart all night
vóonóé'ó to float all night
vóonôhtóvá to sell all night
vóono'eétahe to have sex all night
vóonó'eohtsé to travel by wagon all night
vóonotse'ohe to work all night

To take a sledgehammer to crack a nut

mogi jabeeryuda chogasamgan da taewonda (Korean)
burning your whole house trying to catch a mosquito

tuo kuzi fang pi (Mandarin) to take your trousers off to fart

pire için yorgan yakmak (Turkish) to burn the duvet because of one flea

kee chang jahb thak-a-thaen (Thai) ride an elephant to catch a grasshopper

met een kanon op een mug schieten (Dutch) to shoot a mosquito with a cannon

gubbi mEle bramhAstravE? (Kannada, India) a nuclear weapon on a sparrow?

18.
Animal Magic

hilm il-'utaat kullu firaan (*Arabic*)
the dream of cats is all about mice

When humans looked around them and saw the animals that inhabited their world they often came up with names that described what each animal looked or sounded like, or how it behaved. Among the Amerindian tribes the Navaho word for squirrel is the phrase 'it has a bushy tail' and the word from the Arapaho for elephant is 'it has a bent nose'. The Mingo language was particularly expressive in this regard:

uæhkwëönyö' a peacock (literally, it puts suns all over it)
teyunö'kêôt a sheep (literally, it's got two horns attached)
këötanëhkwi a horse (literally, it hauls logs)
teka'nyakáíte' a mole (literally, both of its hands are slanted)
tewathsistúkwas a firefly (literally, it scatters sparks)
tsyúwë'staka' a seagull (literally, it is known for being around sea-foam)
uthëhtææhtáne' a caterpillar (literally, its fuzz itches)
teyu'skwææt a bull (literally, two standing stones – referring to the bull's testicles)

The great rat with a pocket

Likewise, when Chinese voyagers first saw the kangaroo they described the way it looked to them: **dai shu**, pocket rat, or great rat with a pocket. The Yoruba of West Africa, unused to zebras, called them 'striped horses'. The Indian nations of the Americas were astounded at the sight of the horse when it appeared, brought by the early Spanish conquerors. The Aztecs thought it was a hornless deer. The Sioux named it **shuñka wakãn**, supernatural dog, and the Cheyenne referred to it as **mo-eheno'ha**, domesticated elk. Another animal new to the Cheyenne, the pig, joined their language as **eshkoseesehotame**, dog with sharp nose.

False friends

snog (Danish) grass snake
asp (Pahlavi, Iran) horse
dud (Arabic) caterpillar, worm
formica (Latin) ant
hunt (Estonian) wolf
hunt (Yiddish) dog
lamb (Amharic, Ethiopia) cow

long (Chinese) dragon
moron (Munduruku, Brazil) toad

Fluttering and kicking

Those peoples living closely with animals developed vocabulary to describe all sorts of precisely observed behaviour on land ...

vweluka (Mambwe, Zambia) to jump from branch to branch (said of a monkey)

gigigigigi (Tsonga, South Africa) to stand about dispersed and all looking intently at something in the distance, as cattle seeing a lion

telki (Swahili) the quick ambling gait of a donkey, half walk, half run

thakgantse (Setswana, Botswana) to kick in all directions (as an ox when one leg is held by a thong)

glamarsaich (Gaelic) the noisy lapping (as of a hungry dog)

shebwoso (Potawatomi, USA) a rabbit running fast

... of fish and other creatures at sea:

tekab (Maguindanaon, Philippines) a fish opening its mouth and producing bubbles

siponaina (Yamana, Chile) to go along on the surface of the water and cause a ripple, as fish do

aiagata (Yamana, Chile) to rise up on end and take a deep dive, as the whale when it raises up its flukes

itupi (Mambwe, Zambia) dead fish found floating

hu-q-a (Nuuchahnulth, Canada) a salmon going along with its dorsal fin out of the water

... and of birds and insects on the ground and in the air:

abhinibbijjhati (Pali, India) to break quite through (said of
the chick coming through the shell of the egg)

magaatu (Yamana, Chile) to tuck the head under the wing, as
birds do when composed for sleep

ava-sam-dīna (Sanskrit) the united downward flight of birds

khpa (Dakota, USA) to be wet or clogged, as mosquitos' wings
with dew

tikutamoamo (Gilbertese, Oceania) to alight everywhere (of
a dragonfly)

Scratch, chew, tear, beat

Some actions are common to many creatures:

kwe-swanta (Ganda, Uganda) to lick one's chops when one
has not had enough to eat

kengerhele (Tsonga, South Africa) to stop suddenly in
surprise, be on the alert, as animals hearing a noise

kukuta (Swahili) to shake off water after getting wet, in the
way a bird or dog does

zeula (Kalanga, Botswana) the chewing of animals late at
night

hachistitabatli (Alabama, USA) to beat the tail on the ground

imba (Mambwe, Zambia) to tear away the prey from one
another, as animals fighting over food

Wriggle, wriggle

There are words for sounds too, even those surely heard only by those who live cheek by jowl with the fauna of the world:

pasáw (Tagalog, Philippines) the noise of fish wriggling in the water

rerejat (Iban, Sarawak and Brunei) the noise made by a cricket on landing

kíchchu (Tamil) the chirping of birds; the whining of infants

ekkaranam (Tamil) a noise which a bull makes when about to attack another

saratata (Buli, Ghana) the sound and behaviour of running animals (leaving a trail of dust in the air)

tyaka-tyaka (Tsonga, South Africa) the noise of cattle crashing through dry bush

gungurhu-gungurhu-gungurhu (Tsonga, South Africa) to clatter like a rat trapped in a box

andala (Arabic) the song of the nightingale

atit (Arabic) the moaning bray of a camel

inchasàaya (Alabama, USA) a rattlesnake's rattle

Sunday roast

There are words to describe the most detailed aspects of an animal's appearance ...

scory (Scots) the wrinkled texture of a hedgehog's cheeks

gansuthi (Boro, India) the first-grown feather of a bird's wing

kapy-āsa (Sanskrit) the buttocks of an ape

sondi (Pali, India) the neck of a tortoise

sprochaille (Irish) the loose fold of skin between the legs of a turkey

mokadi (Setswana, Botswana) the fat of a bullfrog

kuris (Manobo, Philippines) the fortune of a chicken written in the scales of its feet

Tucked away

... how they store their food:

bráða-hola (Old Icelandic) a hole where the wild beasts carry their prey

wakhedan (Dakota, USA) the places from which squirrels dig up food

achnátus (Karuk, North America) a place where a rat stores its food

tsembetuta (Chichewa, Malawi) a type of mouse known for saving food for the future

indagitagan (Ojibway, North America) the place where a wild animal goes to eat in the woods

Crocodile skid

… even how they behave in specific and group ways:

kekerikaki (Gilbertese, Oceania) a fish which sometimes
swims backwards
teosammul (Estonian) the speed of a snail
atiqtuq (Iñupiat, Inuit) bears going down to the sea
wosdohedan (Dakota, USA) paths made by squirrels in the
grass
pe'mkowe't (Potawatomi, USA) bear tracks in the snow
lantar (Iban, Sarawak and Brunei) the skidmark left on a
riverbank by a boat or crocodile sliding into the water

Wa!

Originally, humans began by treating animals as hostile, to be
hunted, chased away or killed:

phongoloxa (Tsonga, South Africa) to throw stones or sticks
at an animal to frighten it away
p'isqeyay (Quechuan, Andes) to scare off birds
khapela (Tsonga, South Africa) to drive animals into another's land so that they may do damage there
bohnaskinyan (Dakota, USA) to make an animal crazy or
furious by shooting
phitsisitse (Setswana, Botswana) to kill an insect by crushing
it between the finger and thumb

Down on the farm

But then came the thought of using certain breeds to their advantage:

nanagi (Rapanui, Easter Island) to mark a chicken as one's property by biting one of its toes

piya (Kalanga, Botswana) to hold a goat's leg under one's knee while milking it

verotouaire (Gallo, France) a woman who helps a boar (**vero**) to copulate with the sow (**tree**)

féauðnu-maðr (Old Icelandic) a man lucky with his sheep

Commanding

With this came a new range of calls and cries:

ouk (British Columbian dialect, Canada) a command to a sledge-dog to turn right

koosi (Buli, Ghana) to call chickens by smacking one's tongue

cethreinwr (Welsh) someone who walks backwards, in front of an ox, prompting it with a combination of a song and a sharp stick

To the hand

The Scots, in particular, have a fine collection of animal instructions:

irrnowt a shepherd's call to his dog to pursue cattle
who-yauds a call to dogs to pursue horses
iss a call to a dog to attack
hut a call to a careless horse
re a call to a horse to turn to the right
shug a call to a horse to come to the hand

Animals online

In these days of intense email use, it seems amazing that there is still no official name for @. It is generally called the 'at' symbol. Other languages have come up with all kinds of mostly animal nicknames. Polish calls it **malpa**, monkey; in Afrikaans it is **aapstert**, monkey's tail; in German it is **Klammeraffe**, clinging monkey; and in Dutch it is **apeklootje**, little monkey's

Aw, aw !

As does the Pashto language of Afghanistan and Pakistan:

drhey	when addressing sheep
eekh eekh	when addressing camels
asha asha	when addressing donkeys
aw aw	when addressing oxen
tsh tsh	when addressing horses
kutsh kutsh	when addressing dogs

testicle. The Finns and Swedes see it as a cat curled up with its tail. Swedish has **kattsvans**, and Finnish has at least three names for this idea: **kissanhäntä**, cat tail, **miaumerkki**, meow sign, and **miukumauku**, which means something like meow-meow. In French, Korean, Indonesian, Hebrew and Italian it's a snail. In Turkish (**kulak**) and Arabic (**uthun**) it's an ear, in Spanish it's an elephant's ear (**elefantora**), in Danish it's an elephant's trunk (**snabel**), and elsewhere:

zavinac (Czech) pickled herring
xiao lao-shu (Taiwanese) little mouse
kukac (Hungarian) worm or maggot
sobachka (Russian) little dog
papaki (Greek) duckling
grisehale (Norwegian) curly pig's tail
kanelbulle (Swedish) cinnamon roll
gül (Turkish) rose

How to count on your chickens

In the Gallo dialect in France there is some very specific vocabulary about ensuring that there are always enough eggs:

un anijouet an egg left in a hen's nest to encourage it to lay more in the same place

chaponner to stick a finger up a chicken's bottom to see if it is laying an egg

Man's best friend

It's hardly surprising that that species thought of as closest to humans is described in the most loving detail:

agkew (Manobo, Philippines) to try to snatch food which is hung up out of reach (said of a dog)

manàntsona (Malagasy, Madagascar) to smell or sniff before entering a house, as a dog does

ihdaśna (Dakota, USA) to miss in biting oneself, as a dog trying to bite its own tail

kwiiua-iella (Yamana, Chile) to bite and leave, as a dog does with a strong animal it cannot kill

amulaw (Bikol, Philippines) the barking of dogs in pursuit of game

Roof-gutter rabbit

Our second favourite animal is less loyal and more selfish, but brings us luck if it crosses our path:

lapin de gouttière (French) a cat (literally, roof-gutter rabbit)

echafoureré (Gallo, France) a tickled cat hiding under a table or chair

bilāra-nissakkana (Pali, India) large enough for a cat to creep through

amotóm (Cheyenne, USA) to carry something in the mouth (said especially of a mother cat)

bvoko (Tsonga, South Africa) to spring unsuccessfully at or after, as a cat springs at a mouse which just saves itself

Gee gee

Next up has to be the one that has always helped us get around, and has also let us experience speed, excitement and other less welcome sensations:

asvatthāma (Sanskrit) having the strength of a horse

lekgetla (Setswana, Botswana) the droop of the ears of a tired horse

dzádintsu (Telugu, India) to flap about as a horse does his tail, to reprove by speech

cagailt (Gaelic) a roll of chewed grass in a horse's mouth

ibiihokcho (Alabama, USA) to pass gas in someone's face (as a horse will)

Moo

Fourth on our list is free to roam in India, enjoying its sacred status, while elsewhere it offers sustenance of more than one kind:

kárámpasu (Tamil) a cow whose udder is black, held in great esteem by the Hindus

nyakula (Lozi, Niger-Congo) to try to untie itself by kicking (as a cow tied up by its legs)

silehile (Lozi, Niger-Congo) to besmirch with dung the teats of a cow which refuses to be milked, in order to keep its calf away

deothas (Gaelic) the longing or eagerness of a calf for its mother

clardingo (Welsh) to flee in panic from a warble-fly (said of a herd of cows)

gokuradiya (Sinhala, Sri Lanka) the water in a hole made by a cow's hoof

Drinking twice

We rarely see our fifth and last away from a zoo or safari park, but in the wild this creature certainly lives up to the poet's description as 'Nature's great masterpiece':

dvi-pa (Sanskrit) an elephant (literally, drinking twice – with his trunk and his mouth)

gagau (Malay) an elephant picking up with its trunk

polak (Hindi) straw tied to the end of a bamboo stick which is used to frighten and restrain a furious elephant

isīkā (Sanskrit) an elephant's eyeball

tun-mada (Sinhala, Sri Lanka) an elephant in rut, alluding to the three liquids which exude from him in the rutting season, namely from his temples, his eyes and his penis

Flying low

And then there are those others that we admire, but generally only from a distance:

arspag (Gaelic) the largest seagull

tihunyi (Tsonga, South Africa) a crested cuckoo which sings before the rains and reminds people to collect firewood

jimbi (Luvale, Zambia) a bird which does not yet sing

sarad (Manobo, Philippines) to fly low, at about the height of a coconut palm

Don't count your chickens before they're hatched

Swahili advises us not to curse the crocodile before we've crossed the river and there are all kinds of similar warnings from around the world about not being too hasty:

mithl ilh yibi' samak fi al bahar (Arabic) it's like selling fish still in the sea

man skal ikke sælge skindet, før bjørnen er skudt (Danish) one should not sell the fur before the bear has been shot

älä nuolaise ennen kuin pöydällä tipahtaa (Finnish) don't start licking it up before it drops onto the table

guthimba ti kuura (Kikuyu, Kenya) having rain clouds is not the same as having rain

na neroden Petko kapa mu skroile (Macedonian) they sewed a hat to Peter who is not born yet

tsiplyat po oseni schitayut (Russian) one should count chicks in autumn

ne govori gop, poka ne pereskochish (Russian) don't say hop until you jumped over

ino manga ondjupa ongombe inaayi vala (Ndonga, Namibia) don't hang the churning calabash before the cow has calved

non dire gatto se non l'hai nel sacco (Italian) never say 'cat' if you have not got it in your sack

dereyi görmeden paçaları sıvama (Turkish) do not roll up your trouser legs before you see the stream

19.
Climate Change

gode ord skal du hogge i berg, de
dårligere i snø (*Norwegian*)
carve your good words in stone, the bad in snow

Tiwilight

The world goes round, and at innumerable different times, the day begins. Down in the Antipodes, the Tiwi people of northern Australia describe the sequence before the sun finally appears:

arawunga early morning before dawn
tokwampari early morning when birds sing
yartijumurra darkness before daylight
wujakari first light before sunrise

The dawn chorus

The Hungarians have a specific word – **hajnalpir** – for the first blush of dawn; the Japanese distinguish **ariake**, dawn when the moon is still showing; while the German word **Morgengrauen** (literally, morning greying) describes both the horror of the morning and its grey and sunless colour.

Sun's up

In the Dakota language of the USA, the moon is **hangyetuwi**, the night-sun. Come dawn it can no longer compete with **anpetuwi**, the day-sun:

glukocharazo (Greek) to glow in the dawn light
tavanam (Tamil) the heat of the sun
amaśtenaptapta (Dakota, USA) the glimmering of vapour in the sun's heat
greigh (Gaelic) the uncommon heat of the sun after bursting out from behind a cloud

Weather report

Ah, that famous topic, food for hundreds of thousands of conversations every day. And we are not alone in observing and describing its many moods:

pestpokkenweer (Dutch) dirty rotten weather

dul'avā (Virdainas, Baltics) fog with drizzle

cilala (Bemba, Zambia) the dry spell in a rainy season

boule (Scots) a gap, break; an opening in the clouds betokening fine weather

Postkartenwetter (German) the kind of weather that is too wonderful to be real (literally, postcard weather)

Heat haze

The secondary meanings of weather terms are often very evocative of the climate they describe. For instance, the Scots description of heat haze – **summer-flaws** – is also used for a swarm of gnats dancing in the air; while the Yamana of Chile **unda-tu** also describes the wavy appearance of the air seen over a fire.

The wind of change

Beautifully still conditions never last for long, certainly not in this country:

pew (Scots) the least breath of wind or smoke; the least ripple on the sea

sivisivivi (Mailu, Papua New Guinea) marks on water of a coming wind

kacee (Tsonga, South Africa) to feel a breeze or smell coming towards one

fuaradh-froik (Gaelic) the breeze preceding a shower

False friends

dim (Bosnian) smoke
estate (Italian) summer
lung (Sherpa, Nepal) air
santa (Bosnian) iceberg
tall (Arabic) hill, elevation

Storm warning

We can always sense that moment when things are on the turn:

oi (Vietnamese) to be sultry, muggy, hot and sticky
tvankas (Virdainas, Baltics) stuffy air
bingo (Chewa, South East Africa) the distant roll of thunder
gwangalakwahla (Tsonga, South Africa) a thunderclap is
    very near
kixansiksuya (Dakota, USA) to know by one's feelings that
    unpleasant weather is due

Sunshine shower

After the storm, the rain is lighter, subtler; indeed, it may not be clear quite what's going on:

tmoq yungay (Aboriginal Tayal, Taiwan) a light rain (literally,
    monkey piss)
fa-fa-fa (Tsonga, South Africa) to fall in a shower of drops
mvula-tshikole (Venda, South Africa) rain with sunshine
ördög veri a feleségét (Hungarian) the devil is hitting his
    wife (usually said when the sun is shining but rain is falling
    at the same time)
bijregenboog (Dutch) a secondary rainbow

In a flood

Down on the ground, everything changes:

douh (Somali) a dry watercourse which turns into a fast-moving stream after every downpour

calalalala (Tsonga, South Africa) to come down, as a river in a flood; a glitter (of a large expanse of water or an army with polished weapons)

túvánam (Tamil) rain driven by the wind through the doors or windows

zolilinga (Luvale, Zambia) the watermark made by rain (as on a wooden door)

Soaking up the weather

And all kinds of fun can be had:

edtimbulan (Maguindanaon, Philippines) to walk in the rain

wadlopen (Dutch) to walk sloshing through seamud

chokok (Malay) to splash water in fun

dynke (Norwegian) the act of dunking somebody's face in snow

kram snø (Norwegian) snow which is sticky (excellent for making snowballs and snowmen)

You fish on your side…

Several places in Norway and Sweden are simply called Å. It means river in various Scandanavian languages, but that's all the name tells us about them. But if you go for something rather longer, an awful lot of information can be contained in a name. For instance, Webster Lake in Massachussetts, USA, is also known as

Chargoggagoggmanchauggauggagoggchaubunagunga-maugg

which was a native word for a neutral fishing place near a boundary, a meeting and fishing spot shared by several tribes. A popular interpretation is: 'You fish on your side, I fish on my side, nobody fishes in the middle.' The longest placename still in regular use is for a hill in New Zealand. The ninety-letter Maori name

Taumatawhakatangihangakoauaotamateaurehaeaturi-pukapihimaungahoronukupokaiwhenuaakitana-rahu

means 'The brow of the hill where Tamatea, the man with the big knees, who slid, climbed and ate mountains, the great traveller, sat and played on the flute to his beloved.'

Compass comparisons

The sun features strongly in how other cultures have described the compass points. The Mingo of the USA describe north as **te'kææhkwææhkö**, the sun isn't there; and west as **hekææhk-wë's**, the sun habitually drops down over there. The Bambara people of Mali have more complicated associations:

EAST is the colour white; the land of the dead and of wild and domestic animals.

WEST is the land of the 'sunset people' and of birds; the source of custom and of all goodness and loveliness.

NORTH is identified with the seventh heaven, a far distant country, the dwelling of the great god Faro, who created the world in all its present form; the north is the home of all water creatures – fish, crocodiles and frogs.

SOUTH is peopled by plants and the evil beings whom Faro was forced to destroy at the beginning of time, because they had stolen speech from him; the home of pollution.

Coucher de soleil

Rain or shine, windy or still, the sun sinks down towards the horizon, and the day winds towards its close:

tainunu (Gilbertese, Oceania) the time when shadows lengthen in the late afternoon

pakupaku (Rapanui, Easter Island) to come down in a straight line like the rays of the sun

sig (Sumerian, Mesopotamia) the colour of the low setting sun (reddish-yellow or gold)

iltarusko (Finnish) sunset glow

ahiahi-ata (Rapanui, Easter Island) the last moments of light before nightfall

Silver goddess

Darkness falls, and the night-sun reappears, bringing with it mystery and magic:

jyótsnā (Sanskrit) a moonlight night

yakmoez (Turkish) the effect of moonlight sparkling on water

kuunsilta (Finnish) the long reflection of the moon when it is low in the sky and shining on the calm surface of a lake (literally, moon bridge)

hasi istitta-ammi (Alabama, USA) to bathe one's face in the moon, wash the face four times in moonlight

It's raining cats and dogs

ou vrouens met knopkieries reen (Afrikaans) it's raining old women with clubs

padají trakaře (Czech) it's raining wheelbarrows

det regner skomagerdrenge (Danish) it's raining shoemakers' apprentices

het regent pijpenstelen (Dutch) it's raining pipestems

baron mesleh dobeh asb mirized (Persian) it's raining like the tail of the horse

brékhei kareklopódara (Greek) it's raining chair legs

il pleut comme vache qui pisse (French) it's raining like a pissing cow

es regnet Schusterbuben (German) it's raining young cobblers

estan lloviendo hasta maridos (Spanish) it's even raining husbands

20.
The Root of All Evil

ahjar habib fis-suq minn mitt
skud fis-senduq (*Maltese*)
*a friend in the market is better than one
hundred gold coins in the chest*

A frog's armpit

'Don't offer me advice, give me money,' say the Spanish – and who would disagree, certainly if they're in a tight spot financially:

> **mas limpio que sobaco de rana** (Venezuelan Spanish)
>   broke (literally, cleaner than a frog's armpit)

> **auf den Hund kommen** (German) to be broke (literally, to
>   get to the dog; in medieval times, a dog was painted on the
>   bottom of money chests – if you could see the dog, you had
>   run out of money)
> **n'avoir plus un radis** (French) to be stone broke (literally, to
>   be without a single radish)
> **kukla** (Russian) a roll of bills in which the inner bills have
>   been replaced by worthless paper (literally, a doll)

Cutting gold

Most of us would be more than happy with an easy escape from such an unfortunate predicament:

gaji buta (Malay) getting paid without having to work
att skära guld med täljkniv (Swedish) to make money with
very little effort (literally, to cut gold with a pocket knife)
dawo (Yoruba, Nigeria, Benin and Togo) to produce money by
magic

Gifted

While others find different ways to stay afloat:

pakimkím (Tagalog, Philippines) money given by a godparent
hustrulon (Swedish) a wife's salary
namidakin (Japanese) a small amount of consolation money
(literally, tear money)
pujo (Korean) a congratulatory gift or condolence money

Up against it

It's certainly true that the folding stuff can be elusive; and the occasion when you really need it may be the one time you are unable to find it:

ipatapata (Lozi, Niger-Congo) to try hard to find money with
which to make an urgent purchase
lukupu (Mambwe, Zambia) to miss gaining riches by a
narrow margin

On the floor

When you do finally get some, for heaven's sake be careful with it:

pagar el piso (Chilean Spanish) to take out all your friends and pay with the first pay packet from your new job (literally, to pay for the floor)

madyelakhwirhini (Tsonga, South Africa) a man who immediately spends all he earns and sends nothing home; a spendthrift

peaglatata (Dakota, USA) to exhaust one's own supply by giving to others

It's the thought that counts

To demonstrate their wealth, the Kwakiutl Indians of Vancouver Island destroyed it. Their chiefs publicly burned food, blankets, canoes and ornaments in the ceremony of **potlatch**, a word that means 'giving'. A **potlatch** might be held for a variety of reasons, which varied from group to group, but included puberty rites and death commemorations. It involved a great feast at which the host lavishly distributed valuable property to all the assembled guests. The hitch was that the guests had to reciprocate at some future date – with interest of up to 100 per cent.

An umbrella at midnight

Two proverbs from the Kannada language of Southern India speak eloquently of the paradoxes of getting rich. **HalliddAga kaDle illa; kaDle iddAga hallilla** – there are no nuts when one has teeth and there are no teeth when there are nuts; in other words, when you are young you have no money, and when you have money the chance of enjoying it is often gone. But perhaps this is all as it should be. For the second proverb points up the absurdity of some people's behaviour when they are in a fit state to enjoy their money: **Aishwarya bandre ardha rAthrili koDe hiDkonDa** – when a poor fellow gets rich, he has an umbrella over his head at midnight; which is to say that a newly wealthy man will flaunt the symbol of the well-off, a parasol to shield him from the sun, even in the dark.

False friends

Reformhaus (German) health food store

top (Dutch) done! agreed! it's a bargain!

stershit (Albanian) to sell everything that one has

Detail (German) retail

hamstring (Swedish) hoarding (derives from hamster)

male (Italian) bad, wicked

Cowherd's cake

Sometimes the destitute may just have to make do with a payment in kind:

legopelo (Setswana, Botswana) a piece of meat that is given to someone who has helped skin a cow

angauriyā (Hindi) a ploughman making use of a farmer's plough instead of receiving wages in money or kind

bonnach-iomanach (Gaelic) a cowherd's cake (a special reward for good herding at calving time)

matao ni bwe (Gilbertese, Oceania) the price paid in fish for the loan of a canoe or fishing net

To see thirty-six candles

The French refer to many things in terms of the number thirty-six:

j'ai trente-six choses à faire I have many things to do

tous les trente-six du mois once in a blue moon (literally, each thirty-sixth of the month)

faire les trente-six volontés de quelqu'un to be at someone's beck and call (literally, to do the thirty-six wills of someone)

voir trente-six chandelles to see stars after getting hit on the head (literally, to see thirty-six candles)

Stall

'**Gol' na vydumku khitra**,' say the Russians – poverty is crafty; and it's surely true that having no money can become the spur for entrepreneurial activity, even of the most basic kind:

bahu (Bugotu, Solomon Islands) to barter food for money

ditan (Chinese) a street vendor's stand (with the goods spread out on the ground)

higgler (Jamaican creole) a person selling fruit and vegetables by the roadside

gujrī (Hindi) a roadside market set up in the late afternoons

sitoa (Gilbertese, Oceania) a small trading ship whose decks are set up as stores

chelnoki (Russian) shuttle traders (who buy goods from the back of lorries)

limpiaparabrisas (Mexican Spanish) street kids who gather at intersections with traffic lights and rush to wash the windscreen of cars waiting for the lights to change and then demand to be paid

Red shells out, white shells back

The Kiriwina of the Trobriand Islands in the Pacific have an elaborate gift exchange system called the **kula**. The islanders set off round the islands in large, ocean-going canoes and trade red shell necklaces (**veigun**) in a clockwise direction, and white shell bracelets (**mwali**) in an anti-clockwise direction. The round trip is several hundred miles.

The art of selling

There's a lot of skill (even magic) in encouraging people to part with their hard-earned dosh:

spruik (Australian slang) to talk to attract customers; to hold forth like a showman

verlierlen (Yiddish) to lose a customer to a fellow salesman

vparivat' (Russian) to palm off defective goods

fare orecchie da mercante (Italian) pretending not to understand (literally, to have a merchant's ears)

palulud (Maguindanaon, Philippines) a charm that is supposed to have the power to attract customers

Smoke and mirrors

Although the further up the scale you go, the less need you have for actual goods:

muhaqala (Arabic) the sale of grain while still in growth, dealing in grain futures

dymoprodukt (Russian) an advertised product that is not yet being produced (literally, smoke product)

wheeler (Scots) one who bids at an auction simply to raise the price

One-armed bandit

There are, of course, other ways of making money, if you're prepared to take a chance:

agi (Maranao, Philippines) to win continually in gambling

airi (Maranao, Philippines) to bet again on a card which has just won

an non (Vietnamese) to quit gambling as soon as one has won

balato (Tagalog, Philippines) money given away by a winning gambler as a sign of goodwill

Losers

However, even the most hardened practitioners know that in the long run the betting tables don't pay. As the Germans say, 'Young gamblers, old beggars':

borona (Malagasy, Madagascar) having nothing with which to pay money lost in betting

biho (Maranao, Philippines) a bet, money asked for from winners by losers

pelasada (Maranao, Philippines) the percentage taken from bets by the owner of a gambling place

Tokyo tricks

The Japanese have two words to describe what happens as the temptation to cheat gets stronger:

dakko the flicking movement of the palm that will send goods up into the sleeve

dosa a player with an exceptionally bad hand who will flick a compromising card up his sleeve and quickly substitute a more favourable one

Retail therapy

So what to do with it when you finally have it? Why, hit the streets, of course; and this is an occupation, if not an art, in itself:

faire du lèche-vitrines (French) to go window-shopping (literally, to lick windows)

chokuegambo (Japanese) the wish that there were more designer-brand shops on a given street; the desire to buy things at luxury brand shops

arimuhunán (Tagalog, Philippines) something worth taking although not needed

emax (Latin) fond of buying

You're safer with prison

What a fine array of products the world has in its shop window:

Atum Bom Portuguese tinned tuna
Bimbo Mexican biscuits
Kevin French aftershave
Polio Czech detergent
Vaccine Dutch aftershave
Flirt Austrian cigarettes
Meltykiss Japanese chocolate
Climax Kenyan disinfectant
Hot Piss Japanese antifreeze spray
Naked New Zealand fruit and nut bar
Noisy French butter
Last Climax Japanese tissues
Happy Swedish chocolate
Prison Ugandan body spray

As easy as falling off a log

så let som at klø sig i nakken (Danish) as easy as scratching the back of your neck

semudah membalikkan telapak tangan (Indonesian) as easy as turning your palm around

facile come bere un bicchier d'acqua (Italian) as easy as drinking a glass of water

asameshi mae (Japanese) before breakfast (something that's so easy, you could finish it before breakfast)

nuwoseo tdeokmeokki (Korean) lying on one's back and eating rice cakes

tereyağýndan kýl çeker gibi (Turkish) as if pulling a strand of hair from butter

ežiku ponjatno (Russian) understandable to a hedgehog

21.
The Criminal Life

le diable chie toujours au même
endroit (*French*)
the devil always shits in the same place

Tea leaf

Why work, or even gamble for that matter, when there are far easier ways of enriching yourself?

lipoushka (Russian) a stick with a gluey end for stealing money from a counter (literally, flypaper)

butron (Spanish) a type of jacket with inner pockets worn by shoplifters

levare le scarpe (Italian) to steal the tyres from a car (literally, to take someone else's shoes off)

rounstow (Scots) to cut off the ears of a sheep, and so obliterate its distinctive marks of ownership

---

False friends

bait (Arabic) incentive or motive

egg (Norwegian, Swedish) knife edge

gulp (Afrikaans) to slit, gush, spout

guru (Japanese) a partner in crime

plaster (Hebrew) deceitful or fraudulent

roof (Dutch) robbery

Gangland

Although once you step over that line, who knows what company you may be forced to keep:

ladenlichter (Dutch) a till-robber

pisau cukur (Malay) a female hustler who cons men into giving her money

harza-duzd (Persian) someone who steals something of no use to him or anyone else

adukalipewo (Mandinka, West Africa) a highway robber (literally, give me the purse)

belochnik (Russian) a thief specializing in stealing linen off clothes lines (this was very lucrative in the early 1980s)

Scissorhand

Considerable skill, experience and bravado may be required for success:

> **forbice** (Italian) pickpocketing by putting the index and middle fingers into the victim's pocket (literally, scissors)
>
> **cepat tangan** (Malay) quick with the hands (in pickpocketing or shoplifting or hitting someone)
>
> **poniwata** (Korean) a victim who at first glance looks provincial and not worth robbing, but on closer scrutiny shows definite signs of hidden wealth
>
> **komissar** (Russian) a robber who impersonates a police officer

And sometimes even magic:

> **walala** (Luvale, Zambia) a thieves' fetish which is supposed to keep people asleep while the thief steals
>
> **za-koosirik** (Buli, Ghana) a person who transfers the plants of a neighbour's field to his own by magic

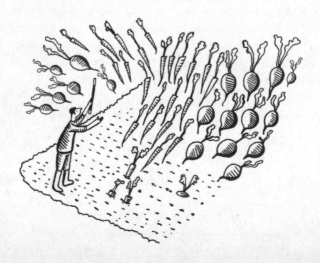

Lost in translation

In their eagerness to move into and conquer new markets, many huge Western companies forgot to do their homework. When the name Microsoft was first translated into Chinese, they went for a literal translation of the two parts of the name which, unfortunately, meant 'small and flaccid'.

Pepsi's famous slogan 'Come Alive with Pepsi' was dropped in China after it was translated as 'Pepsi brings your ancestors back from the grave'.

When American Airlines wanted to advertise its new leather first-class seats in the Mexican market, it translated its 'Fly in Leather' campaign literally, but **vuela en cuero** meant 'Fly Naked' in Spanish.

Colgate introduced in France a toothpaste called **Cue**, the name of a notorious pornographic magazine.

Coca-Cola was horrified to discover that its name was first read by the Chinese as **kekoukela**, meaning either 'bite the wax tadpole' or 'female horse stuffed with wax', depending on the dialect. Coke then researched 40,000 characters to find a phonetic equivalent – **kokou kole** – which translates as 'happiness in the mouth'

Kindling

Their trains and tubes are punctual to the nearest second; equal efficiency seems to characterize those Japanese who take criminal advantage of such crowded environments:

nakanuku, inside pull-out: to carefully slip one's hand into a victim's trouser pocket, draw out the wallet, flick it open, whip out cash and credit cards, close it and slip it back into the victim's trouser pocket

oitore, walking next to a well-dressed victim, plunging a razor-sharp instrument into his attaché case and cutting the side open

okinagashi, put and flow: those who climb on a local train at one station, grab bags and coats, cameras and camcorders, and then jump off at the following station

takudasu, kindle and pull out: to drop, as if by mistake, a lit cigarette into a victim's jacket or open shirt, and then, while the victim is frantically trying to locate the burning butt, come to his aid, helping him unbutton and frisk through jacket, shirt and undershirt, taking the opportunity to lift wallets and other valuables out of pockets and bags

Descending spiders

Nor does this fine vocabulary dry up when describing the activity of Japanese burglars: **maemakuri**, lifting the skirt from the front, means they enter through the front gates; while **shirimakuri**, lifting the skirt from behind, describes entry through a gate or fence at the rear of the house. One obvious hazard is the **gabinta**, the dog, that starts barking or snarling at the intruders (the word literally means 'this animal has no respect for its superiors'). There is only one way to deal with such an obstacle: **inukoro o abuseru**, the deadly pork chop, otherwise known as **shūtome o kudoku**, silencing one's mother-in-law. Once at the door you confront the **mimochi musume**, the lock (literally, the pregnant daughter), who must be handled with the softest of touches, unless of course you are in possession of the **nezumi**, the mice (or master keys).

As for the crooks themselves, they come in all varieties. There is the **sagarigumo**, or descending spider, the man or woman who braves the slippery tiles of the roof to reach their target; the **denshinkasegi**, the telegram breadwinners, who get there by shinning up telephone poles; the **shinobikomi**, thieves who enter crawling; the **odorikomi**, who enter 'dancing', i.e. brash criminals with guns; the **mae**, or fronts, debonair thieves who simply walk up to the main door; or the super-sly **ninkātā**, who leaves no trace: the master thief.

There is the **ichimaimono**, the thief who works alone; and the **hikiai**, those who pull together, i.e. partners in crime. There are **nitchūshi**, broad-daylight specialists, and **yonashi**, night specialists; even **miyashi**, shrine specialists. There are **akisunerai**, empty-nest targeters, those who specialize in targeting unattended houses; **neshi**, sleep specialists, the men who target bedrooms after the loot has been assembled and packed; and even evil **tsukeme**, literally, touching eyes: thieves who barge into bedrooms to rape sleeping victims.

Radish with glasses

Not content with colourful descriptions of robbers, the Japanese have an extensive vocabulary for cops too: there are the **gokiburi**, the cockroaches, policemen on motorcycles, who can follow burglars over pavements and through parks; the **kazaguruma**, the windmill, an officer who circles the streets and alleys, getting closer and closer to the area where the criminals are working; the **daikon megane**, the radish with glasses, the naive young officer who's not going to be a problem for the experienced crook; or the more problematic **oji**, the uncle, the dangerous middle-aged patrolman who knows all the members of the gang by name and is liable to blow the whistle first and ask questions later.

As if that wasn't enough, policemen on those overcrowded islands can also be described as **aobuta** (blue pigs), **en** (monkeys), **etekō** (apes), **karasu** (crows), **aokarasu** (blue crows), **itachi** (weasels), **ahiru** (ducks), **hayabusa** (falcons), **ahōdori** (idiotic birds, or albatrosses), **kē** (dogs), **barori** (Korean for pig), and **koyani** (cat, from the Korean **koyangi**). Officers even turn into insects such as **hachi** (bees), **dani** (ticks), **kumo** (spiders), **mushi** (bugs) and **kejirami** (pubic lice).

When crimes go wrong

'Punishment,' say the Spanish, 'is a cripple, but it arrives.' Criminals may get away with it for a while, but in the end justice of some kind generally catches up with them:

chacha (Korean) the disastrous act of each gang member dashing down a different alley

afersata (Amharic, Ethiopia) the custom, when a crime is committed, of rounding up all local inhabitants in an enclosure until the guilty person is revealed

andare a picco (Italian) to sink (to be wanted by the police)

cizyatiko (Mambwe, Zambia) to make a man believe that he is safe so as to make time for others to arrest him

panier à salade (French) a salad shaker (a police van)

annussāveti (Pali, India) to proclaim aloud the guilt of a criminal

Pig box

All except the perpetrator are happy to see that anyone taking the immoral shortcut to personal enrichment ends up in a very bad place:

obez' yannik (Russian) a detention ward in a police station (literally, monkey house)

butabako (Japanese) the cooler, clink (literally, pig box)

bufala (Italian) a meat ration distributed in jail (literally, she-buffalo – so called because of its toughness)

Into the pit

And society may exact its just deserts:

gbaa ose (Igbo, Nigeria) to rub in pepper by way of punishment or torture

kitti (Tamil) a kind of torture in which the hands, ears or noses of culprits are pressed between two sticks

dhautī (Sanskrit) a kind of penance (consisting of washing a strip of white cloth, swallowing it and then drawing it out of the mouth)

ráhu-mukhaya (Sinhala, Sri Lanka) a punishment inflicted on criminals in which the tongue is forced out and wrapped in cloth soaked in oil and set on fire

barathrum (Ancient Greek) a deep pit into which condemned criminals were thrown to die

tu-tù (Vietnamese) a prisoner ready for the electric chair

IDIOMS OF THE WORLD

As thick as thieves

vodoi nye pozolyosh (Russian) water can't be separated

aralarindan su sizmaz (Turkish) not even water can pass between them

entendre comme cul et chemise (French) to get along like one's buttocks and shirt

uni comme les doigts de la main (French) tied like the fingers of a hand

una y carne ser como (Spanish)/**como una y mugre** (Mexican Spanish) to be fingernail and flesh/like a fingernail and its dirt

sange paye ghazwin (Persian) as thick as volcanic stone

22.
Realpolitik

em rio que tem piranha, jacaré nada
de costas (*Brazilian Portuguese*)
*in a piranha-infested river, alligators do
backstroke*

Pipe and sunshade

Once upon a time life was straightforward: the chief ran the show and everyone fell in behind:

pfhatla-pfhatla (Tsonga, South Africa) to make a present to the chief to abate his anger

tarriqu-zan (Persian) an officer who clears the road for a prince

chātra (Pali, India) one who carries his master's sunshade

vwatika (Mambwe, Zambia) to place the pipe in the mouth of the chief

kapita mwene (Mambwe, Zambia) the time of the stroll taken by the chief (between 9 and 10 p.m., when everyone had retired, the chief would go about quietly, eavesdropping to find out those talking about him)

magani (Mindanao, Philippines) the custom of obtaining leadership and the right to wear red clothes through killing a certain number of people

tirai (Tamil) a tribute paid by one king to another more powerful

ramanga (Betsileo, Madagascar) a group of men whose business is to eat all the nail-parings and to lick up all the spilt blood of the nobles (literally, blue blood)

mangkat (Indonesian) to die for one's king or queen

A gift

Things weren't so great for those at the bottom of the pile, however interesting their duties:

ravey (Manobo, Philippines) to enslave someone because he didn't obey a command

dapa (Malay) a slave-messenger sent as a gift with a proposal of marriage

dayo (Bikol, Philippines) a slave who stands guard over the grave of a leading member of the community so that the body will not be disinterred by sorcerers

pachal (Malay) a slave of a slave

golamkhana (Bengali) a factory for imbuing people with a slave mentality

False friends

tank (Tocharic, Turkey) to interfere

tilts (Latvian) bridge

Transparent (German) banner, placard

bingo (Kapampangan, Philippines) chip in a blade

doshman (Romani) enemy

exito (Spanish) success

Parole (German) motto, slogan

Changing shirts

Democracy freed us from the old hierarchies and gave us the power to choose our own destinies ...

valboskap (Swedish) ignorant voters (who vote as they are told)

qualunquismo (Italian) an attitude of indifference to political and social issues

apocheirotonesis (Ancient Greek) a rejection by a show of hands

chaquetero (Central American Spanish) someone who changes political ideas as easily as changing shirts

porros (Mexican Spanish) thugs who stand around polling stations and intimidate voters

Full poodle

... with leaders directly answerable to us and our interests:

phak kanmuang (Thai) political parties that become active only during or prior to elections

Politpopper (German) politically correct and correctly dressed (literally, a square politician)

göra en hel Pudel (Swedish) a politician, or some other well-known person who has done something bad, publicly admitting being bad but promising not to do it again and humbly asking for forgiveness (literally, do a full poodle)

Muffled

Perhaps we just have to accept that the political mindset is never going to change that radically:

aincātānī (Hindi) the manipulation and manoeuvring, tugging and pulling, a struggle inspired by selfish motives

ficcarsi (Italian) to get access to a group to gain advantages from them

başına çorap örmek (Turkish) to plot against someone (literally, to knit a sock for the head)

akal bulus (Indonesian) a cunning ploy (literally, a turtle's trick)

akarnok (Hungarian) someone with unscrupulous ambition

Power corrupts

It's commonly accepted that there are all kinds of unofficial extra benefits to being in power. The phrase in the Sinhala language of Sri Lanka for a local member of parliament, **dheshapaalana adhikaari**, also means crook and someone born out of wedlock:

sglaim (Gaelic) a great deal of the good things of life acquired in a questionable way

dedocratico (Spanish) an undemocratic appointment to a governmental position

zalatwic (Polish) using acquaintances to accomplish things unofficially

bal tutan parmağını yalar (Turkish proverb) a person who holds the honey licks his finger (a person given a job involving valuables will gain some benefit for himself)

kazyonnovo kozla za khvost poderzhat – mozhno shubu sshit' (Russian proverb) just even from having once held a state goat's tail one can make a fur coat (i.e. an official can make money by bribes)

Tail between legs

Many everyday English words are derived from other languages. Finding out more about their roots often casts a fascinating new light on the word itself:

accolade derives from the French **accoler** (to embrace) because knighthoods were initially conferred with an embrace

agony comes from the Ancient Greek **agonia** (contest): the athletes in training for the Olympic Games put their bodies through intense discipline to reach the peak of fitness, denying themselves normal pleasures and enduring punishing physical tests

coward comes from the Old French **couard** (tail) and thus we have the image of a dog retreating with its tail between its legs

jargon comes from the Old French word **jargoun** (twittering), the sound made by birds, incomprehensible to others

muscle is descended from the Latin word **musculus** (little mouse), a rather apt description of the moving and changing form under the skin, especially of the arms and legs

Talk box

The language of politics is famous for both **rollo** (Spanish), the long boring speech (literally, a paper roll), and for double speak. All round the world it's very important to listen extremely closely to what politicans say – and to what they don't:

borutela (Tsonga, South Africa) to praise another in his presence but malign him behind his back

feleka (Setswana, Botswana) to speak so as to conceal one's meaning; to be intentionally ambiguous

chíndugirathu (Tamil) to give a sign by pressing with the finger, unobserved by any third party

tok bokkis (Tok Pisin, Papua New Guinea) a way of giving words hidden meanings (literally, talk box)

achakiy (Quechuan, Andes) to say one thing and do something else

Problem solving

The Bambuti people of Congo have no chiefs or formal system of government; problems and disputes are solved by general discussion often involving the use of humour. Elsewhere, people have other ways of achieving agreement:

taraadin (Arabic) a compromise; a way of solving a problem without anyone losing face

mochi (Chinese) the rapport or teamwork that enables people to cooperate smoothly (literally, silent contract)

remettre les pendules à l'heure (French) to re-align something, for example, in establishing who is the boss, or how we work, or anything else (literally, to set the clocks at the right time again)

biritululo (Kiriwani, Papua New Guinea) comparing yams to settle a dispute

War elephants

What a shame that such delightful methods can't be universally employed. But from the start of time dispute-resolution has often been alarmingly violent:

gazi (Mauritanian dialect) a plundering raid in which at least forty camels are employed

falurombolás (Hungarian) the destruction of villages

Schrecklichkeit (German) a deliberate policy of terrorizing non-combatants

edsabil (Maguindanaon, Philippines) to fight until death for the cause of Allah

nuulone (Anywa, Nilo-Saharan) a victory dance with rifles after a war

Cancer forces

All that's changed over the years is the deadliness of the weapons used:

dagadaga (Sranan Tongo, Surinam) a machine gun

plofstof (Afrikaans) explosive (literally, puff/bang stuff)

springstof (Dutch) an explosive (literally, jump matter)

rakovye voiska (Russian) strategic missile forces (literally, cancer forces – referring to the numerous cancerous diseases caused by radiation)

Heroes

On the battlefield itself individuals make extraordinary sacrifices ...

lwa manyanga (Mambwe, Zambia) to fight one another crawling along on all fours

mamakakaua (Hawaiian) the leading man in battle who bears the brunt of the fighting

ohiampunut (Finnish) one who has survived in battle (literally, shot/fired past)

abhí-vīra (Sanskrit) surrounded by heroes

Yellow-bellies

... or not, as the case may be:

ngivhe (Venda, South Africa) to hit with the butt-end of a spear (a blow given as a warning to escape)

rafizat (Persian) a body of soldiers who deserted their commander and retreated

imboscarsi (Italian) to lie in ambush, to evade military service, to avoid working, or to retreat to a secluded place to make love (literally, to take to the woods)

palias (Maranao, Philippines) the power or magic which protects its possessor from a bullet in battle

Handschuhschneeballwerfer (German) somebody who wears gloves to throw snowballs – used in general for all cowards

War trophies

There are no limits to cruelty, savagery and treachery:

liput (Manobo, Philippines) to throw someone off guard, through an appearance of goodwill, in order to kill him

usauara (Yamana, Chile) to shout, as a group of men, when ready to make an assault on someone they intend to kill

áhaneoha'ov (Cheyenne, USA) to kill someone by stepping on him

tsantsa (Jivaro, Ecuador) a human head shrunken and dried as a war trophy

tzompantli (Aztec) a rack of skulls

Legacy

But when it's all over, what are we left with?

aidos (Ancient Greek) the understanding of the need for humility at the point of victory

Gleichgültigkeit (German) the feeling of dreadful moral insensibility and detachment which is a peculiar legacy of wars

Cucumbers and shaving brushes

And, all too often, a large standing army. Who better than the Russians to tell us all about the realities of that sort of organization?

ogourets a soldier in his first six months of service (literally, a cucumber – referring to the colour green, which signifies inexperience)

pomazok a soldier who has served more than one year and is therefore released from certain menial tasks (literally, a shaving brush)

chelovek-amfibiya a soldier on dishwashing duty (literally, an amphibian man)

khoronit' okourok a punishment for soldiers who drop their cigarette butts on the ground; when even one such butt is found all soldiers are woken up in the middle of the night and forced to spend hours digging deep holes to bury individual butts

lekarstvo ot lyubvi two years of army service (literally, a cure for love, meaning that girlfriends rarely wait for soldiers to come home)

Something is rotten in the state of Denmark

hay un gato encerrado (Spanish) there's a cat shut up

les dés sont pipés (French) the dice are cheated

il y a anguille sous roche (French) there is an eel under the rock

iskat' igolku v stoge sena (Russian) there is a needle in the bag

hayya min taht tibn (Arabic) a snake under the hay

23.
From Better
to Hearse

Dios es el que sana, y el medico lleva
la plata (*Spanish*)
*God cures the patient and the doctor pockets
the fee*

Fagged out

We have all kinds of habits that aren't exactly good for us. As the Italian proverb cheerily goes: '**Bacco, tabacco e Venere, riducon l'uomo in cenere**', Bacchus, tobacco and Venus make men into ashes:

Glimmstengel (German) a cigarette (literally, a glowing stick)

pitillo (Spanish) a cigarette (literally, a small whistle)

bychkovat' (Russian) to smoke only part of a cigarette so as to save the butt

sassakisibingweiabas (Ojibway, North America) feeling a burning pain in my eyes from too much smoke

Peaky

The simplest symptoms can announce forthcoming suffering:

hí (Rapanui, Easter Island) to have a headache or to blow one's nose

kirukiruppu (Tamil) dizziness

cloch (Scots) to cough frequently and feebly

koodho (Anywa, Nilo-Saharan) to fart repeatedly

ku-susuukirira (Ganda, Uganda) to feel the first shivers of a fever

svimfardig (Swedish) ready to faint

motami-ella (Yamana, Chile) to go home or to a place eastwards and throw up

Hypo

Some people are more likely to succumb to illness than others:

niba n aoraki (Gilbertese, Oceania) a person very susceptible
  to catching every disease
mabuk darah (Malay) one who becomes sick upon seeing
  blood
wakakhtakeća (Dakota, USA) one who is made sick by a little
  matter, one who is nervous
aráttam (Tamil) the anxiety of a sick person

STD

Love is often described using the terminology of disease, as with
dongai (Fijian) love sickness; while sex is seen both as a cause of
sickness and as a cure:

pham-phòng (Vietnamese) to become sick after having
  intercourse
una cachiaspirina (Chilean Spanish) refers to how one will
  sweat heavily during sex and thus kill a cold

Sweating carrots

All too soon things become more serious:

zweet peentjes (Dutch) sweating like a pig (literally, sweating carrots)

fare i gattini (Italian) to vomit (literally, to make the kittens)

ca-ca-ca (Tsonga, South Africa) to have diarrhoea; to rain heavily

sarar burer (Chorti, Guatemala) a fever accompanied by an itch

útsu (Telugu, India) the falling out of the hair from sickness

oka/shete (Ndonga, Namibia) urination difficulties caused by eating frogs before the rain has duly fallen

kinudegan (Maguindanaon, Philippines) a disease in men that causes the penis to retract inside the body

Quack remedies

Routine must be interrupted and steps must be taken:

krankfeiern (German) to call in sick (literally, to celebrate illness)

tombola (Kalanga, Botswana) to extract a thorn from flesh using a safety pin

tervismuda (Estonian) curative mud

verkwakzalveren (Dutch) to spend money on quack remedies

kudóripannugirathu (Tamil) to slit or cut the top of the head in order to put in medicine to cure dangerous diseases

Docteur, docteur

Few enjoy handing themselves over to doctors, but sometimes it's unavoidable; or, as they say in France, **inévitable**:

> **trente-trois** say ah! (literally, thirty-three – said by a doctor to the patient)
>
> **artilleur de la pièce humide** a male nurse (literally, artilleryman of the wet gun)
>
> **passer sur le billard** to undergo surgery (literally, to go onto the billiard table)

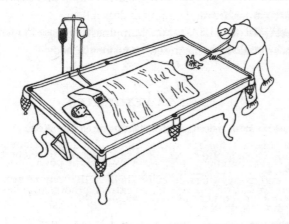

Surgical spirit

In some societies recommended cures may not be primarily medical:

millu (Quechuan, Andes) a rock of aluminium sulphate used by witch doctors, who diagnose illnesses by analysing its colour change when it is thrown into a fire

ti-luoiny (Car, Nicobar Islands) to call on the spirit of a sick man to return

tawák (Tagalog, Philippines) a quack doctor with magic saliva

anavinakárayá (Sinhala, Sri Lanka) a juggler, one who practises incantations upon persons who have been poisoned or bitten by a serpent

iⁿdahli (Alabama, USA) to cut stripe marks on, in order to suck out blood (applied to a hexed or sick person)

Hex

A Chilote Indian, who has gathered up the spittle of an enemy, will put it in a potato, hang it in the smoke, and utter certain spells in the belief that his enemy will waste away as the potato dries in the smoke. And many others, likewise, believe that one person can be responsible for another's physical decline:

khmungha (Dakota, USA) to cause sickness or death in a supernatural way

The devil's in the detail

If it's an evil spirit to blame, it will need to be expelled. Methods differ:

tin-fu-ko (Car, Nicobar Islands) the driving out of the devil from a man by beating the ground with the thick stubs of a coconut leaf

sosela (Tsonga, South Africa) to cure a person by exorcism through the beating of drums

phurbu (Tibetan) ceremonial nails with which evil demons are symbolically nailed fast and banished

Corpse in the middle

The Koreans, Japanese and Chinese (both in Cantonese and Mandarin) avoid the number 4 since in all these languages it has a very similar pronunciation to the word for death. Chinese and Korean buildings often do not have a fourth floor, replacing the number 4 (**sa**) with the letter F. This is not the only number that the Chinese are wary of: the number 1414 is especially avoided because when spoken it sounds just like the words 'definite death, definite death'. Many traditional Chinese people believe that having an uneven number of people in a photograph brings bad luck. To have three people is of greater consequence as the person in the middle will die.

Recuperation

With luck, however outlandish it is, the cure will work and time will do the rest:

mimai (Japanese) to visit a sick person in the hospital

hletela (Tsonga, South Africa) to help a sick person to walk; to lead, as a hen does her chickens

samaya (Maguindanaon, Philippines) a party held to celebrate the promised cure for someone who is sick

iⁿsobáayli (Alabama, USA) to have the feeling come back to a body part

amūlha-vinaya (Pali, India) an acquittal on the grounds of restored sanity

Curtains

But nothing can ever be taken for granted:

doi (Vietnamese) to make one's last recommendations before death

urdhwaswása (Sinhala, Sri Lanka) the rattling in the throat which precedes death

agonia (Spanish) the dying breath

sa-soa (Bakweri, Cameroon) a comb; to make deathbed statements as to the disposition of property

Clogs and slippers

We kick the bucket or turn up our toes. The Russians play the snake, throw their hooves outwards, glue up their slippers, or throw out their best skates. The theme of no longer being shod and upright on your feet is widespread …

estirar la pata (Latin American Spanish) to stretch out your leg

colgar los tenis (Mexican Spanish) to hang up or hand in your tennis shoes

at stille træskoene (Danish) to put aside the clogs

zaklepat bačkorama (Czech) to bang together a pair of slippers

oikaista koipensa (Finnish) to straighten one's shanks

nalları havaya dikmek (Turkish) to raise horse shoes to the sky

… but not exclusive:

gaan bokveld toe (Afrikaans) to go to the goat field

cerrar el paraguas (Costa Rican Spanish) to close the umbrella

liar el petate (Spanish) to roll up the sleeping mat

passer l'arme a gauche (French) to pass the firearm to the left

ins Gras beißen (German) to bite into the grass

a da colţul (Romanian) to turn around the corner

hälsa hem (Swedish) to send home one's regards

irse al patio de los callados (Chilean Spanish) to go to the courtyard of the hushed

ya kwanta dama (Hausa, Nigeria) he is lying on his right arm (Muslims are buried not lying on their backs but on the right arm facing the Kaabah)

A thousand cuts

To die of an illness is not ideal, but in comfortable surroundings, with loved ones around us, perhaps better than some of the alternatives:

lepur (Malay) to die through suffocation in mud

asa (Korean) death from starvation

áhano'xéohtsé (Cheyenne, USA) to die from carrying a load

skeelah (Hebrew) stoning to death

lang-trì (Vietnamese) death by a thousand cuts (an ancient punishment)

prayopaveshī (Hindi) one who undertakes a fast unto death

chŏngsa (Korean) love suicide, double suicide

fwa imfwa leza (Mambwe, Zambia) to die abandoned and alone (without having anyone to fold one's arms and legs for the burial)

lavu (Manobo, Philippines) to drown someone by overturning their canoe

Another way to go

The Fore tribe of New Guinea suffer from a terrible disease called **kuru**, which means shaking death. It is also known as the laughing sickness from the disease's second stage in which the sufferers laugh uncontrollably. It has a 100 per cent fatality rate.

Stiff

There's no saving us now; the best we can hope for is a little dignity:

tlanyi (Tsonga, South Africa) to find a person lying dead when one thought him alive

bahk' e chamen (Chorti, Guatemala) the fright caused by looking at a corpse

kreng (Dutch) a dead body which is bloated from being submerged in water for a substantial period of time (also a bitch)

gruz 200 (Russian) corpses transported by air (literally, load 200)

False friends

arm (Estonian) scar
cocoa (Nahuatl, Mexico) to suffer pain
halal (Hungarian) death
kill (Amharic, Ethiopia) skull
kiss (Swedish) pee
men (Thai) a bad smell
rib (Somali) contraction
rat (Romani) blood
safari (Zarma, Nigeria) medicine
wish (Bashgali, India) poison; medicine

Feet first

Every culture attaches importance to a respectful disposal of the dead; but *how* exactly they do it is different all over:

vynosit' (Russian) to bury someone (literally, to carry someone out feet first)

monoklautos (Ancient Greek) with one mourner

tomboka (Luvale, Zambia) to dance (said of an executioner)

sahagamanamu (Telugu, India) the burning alive of a widow, with her dead husband

Leichenschmaus (German) the meal after the funeral (literally, corpse banquet)

xuxo (Tsonga, South Africa) the spot where an important man died; when rites are observed for his spirit, people go first to that place, then to his grave

Funeral crashers

'A beautiful funeral does not necessarily lead to paradise,' runs a Creole proverb and, were we still able to care, such a thought might be reassuring:

tumeakana (Yamana, Chile) to not show the grief for a friend who has died that is expected from relatives, to act when a mourner as though one was not a mourner

pesamenteiro (Portuguese) one who habitually joins groups of mourners at the home of a deceased person, ostensibly to offer condolences but in reality to partake of the refreshments which he expects will be served

In loving memory

Now all that's left is for those who remain to remember and express their feelings:

di-huong (Vietnamese) the memory of a dead lover

keriah (Hebrew) a tear in clothes to signify a broken heart

miàti-drànomàso (Malagasy, Madagascar) to go up to the palace to weep on the decease of the sovereign

nyekar (Indonesian) to visit and lay flowers on the grave of a dead relative or friend

prātahsmaranīya (Hindi) worthy of being remembered every morning; revered

yortsayt (Yiddish) the anniversary of someone's death

Hex revenge

While some love and remember, there are others who believe that if someone is ill and dies there must be someone to blame; and appropriate action may have to be taken:

> **rihehlo** (Tsonga, South Africa) a spell cast upon a person by putting medicines on the grave of one killed by his witchcraft

Radish tips

Once under the ground we say we are 'pushing up daisies'. For the French, though, to be dead and buried is either **engraisser les asticots**, fattening the maggots, or **manger les pissenlits par la racine**, eating dandelions by the roots. Even more imaginatively the Germans have **sich die Radieschen von unten angucken**, he's looking at the radishes from below.

Out of the frying pan and into the fire

min taht al dalf lataht al mizrab (Arabic) from under the
drip to under the spout

dostat se z bláta do louıe (Czech) out of the mud into the
puddle

aasmaan se gire khajoor mein atke (Hindi) down from the
skies into the date tree

takut akan lumpur lari ke duri (Indonesian) afraid of mud,
escape to thorns

sudah jatuh tertimpa tangga pula (Indonesian) already
fallen and hit by the stairs as well

lepas dari mulut harimau masuk ke mulut buaya
(Indonesian) freed from the tiger's mouth to enter the
crocodile's mouth

iz ognya da v polymya (Russian) from fire to flame

yağmurdan kaçarken doluya yakalanmak (Turkish)
caught by the hail while running away from the rain

24.
The Great Beyond

człowiek strzela, Pan Bóg kule nosi
(*Polish*)
man shoots, God carries the bullets

So where do we go once the body has been burned, buried or, as with the Zoroastrian Parsees of India, pecked off the skeleton by vultures? It's hard for us to believe that the particular vitality that once animated the face of a loved one hasn't gone somewhere:

hanmdohdaka (Dakota, USA) to tell of one's intercourse with the spiritual world, to speak unintelligibly

dagok (Malay) clouds on the horizon of weird and changing form (believed to be ghosts of murdered men)

beina-fœrsla (Old Icelandic) the removal of bones (from one churchyard to another)

Fancy meeting you again

For Hindus, Buddhists and Native Americans, among others, the afterlife is not necessarily another place:

gatâgati (Sanskrit) going and coming, dying and being born again

púsápalan panninavan (Tamil) one who in the present life receives the reward of merit acquired in a former state

apagabbha (Pali, India) not entering another womb (i.e. not destined for another rebirth)

tihanmdeya (Dakota, USA) to have been acquainted in a former state of existence

Just a jealous guy

For others, the spirits of the dead may well stick around and remain animate enough to be called on in times of need:

hanmde (Dakota, USA) to have intercourse with the spirit world

zangu (Luvale, Zambia) a dance to immunize an adulterous woman to the spirit of her dead husband

ngar (Kaurna Warra, Australia) the call of a dead person

kuinyo (Kaurna Warra, Australia) the voice of the dead

andoa (Bakweri, Cameroon) to invoke spirits by spitting out the juice of leaves

havu (Bugotu, Solomon Islands) to make an offering to a ghost

False friends

sad (Sanskrit) being
pop (Bosnian) priest
bigot (French) sanctimonious
eleven (Hungarian) the living
fun (Lao) dream
hell (Norwegian) luck

Holy cockerel

Sometimes mere spirits aren't enough and stronger supernatural agents have to be called on. Many and varied are the prayers and rituals offered to the world's deities:

kahók (Tagalog, Philippines) the act of dipping fingers in holy water

a-cāmati (Sanskrit) to sip water from the palm of one's hand for purification

hacer (se) cruces (Latin American Spanish) to cross yourself in the hope that God will help you to understand.

thì thup (Vietnamese) to go down on one's knees then get up again, to make repeated obeisances

kiam (Malay) to stand during prayer

anda (Latin American Spanish) a wooden frame for carrying images of saints in processions

miau (Iban, Sarawak and Brunei) to wave a cockerel over a person while uttering a prayer

Broken sewing needles

Many and varied too are the building of their shrines and how they are decorated:

abhi-gamana (Sanskrit) the act of cleansing and smearing with cowdung the way leading to the image of the deity

laplap bilong alta (Tok Pisin, Papua New Guinea) an altar cloth

hari kuyo (Japanese) a shrine for broken sewing needles (out of respect for the tools of the sewing trade)

tintueta-wen (Buli, Ghana) the personal god of a living or dead person whose shrine has not yet been transferred to the front of the house

bìt torng lǎng prá (Thai) doing a good deed in secret (literally, pasting gold leaf onto the back of the Buddha image)

One who understands

In most cultures, one spirit stands pre-eminent above all others and is always the One to be both consulted and worshipped:

Hawëníyu' (Mingo, USA) God (literally, he is the one whose word/voice is good)

olumonron (Yoruba, Nigeria, Benin and Togo) one who understands people's problems, God

Candle cormorant

'He who is near the church is often far from God,' say the French; and there is always a risk of substituting religiosity for virtue:

hywl (Welsh) religious or emotional fervour, as experienced with preaching, poetry reading, sporting events, etc.

une grenouille de bénitier (French) an extremely devout churchwoman (literally, a frog of the holy-water basin)

Kerzlschlucker (Austrian German) an insufferably pious person who never misses a mass (literally, a candle cormorant)

On a hedgehog's back

The English language is full of relics of our former, more religious days. The expression 'crikey' is a truncation of the oath 'by Christ's key' and 'bloody' of 'by our Lady'. Socrates swore **ni ton kuna**, by the dog; and Pythagoras is said to have sworn **ma tin tetrakton**, by the number four. Even atheistic Baudelaire swore by the sacred St Onion. The following expressions of astonished disbelief are just as outlandish:

Kors i taket! (Swedish) Cross in the ceiling! (used when something rare happens)

Toushite svet, vynosite chemodany! (Russian) Switch off the light and take out your suitcases! (used when something is a great surprise)

Holla die Waldfee! (German) Ooh, the forest's fairy! (exclamation of surprise, often with an ironic connotation)

In groppa al riccio! (Italian) On a hedgehog's back! (the response to which is **Con le mutande di ghisa!**, Wearing underpants made of cast iron!)

Sounds better

Japanese monks invented pious euphemisms so as not to taint the inner sanctum with jarring worldly words. Whipping came to be called **nazu** (caressing), tears **shiotaru** (dropping salt), money **moku** (eyes), testicles **ryōgyaku** (spiritual globes), and toilets **kish-isho** (a place of truth).

Charismatic

However much some would prefer it if none of us believed in anything, it seems that holy men (and women) are here to stay:

vusitavant (Pali, India) one who has reached perfection (in chaste living)

mana (Polynesian dialect) the spiritual charisma attributed to holy people

samádhi (Tamil) the abstract contemplation of an ascetic, in which the soul is considered to be independent of the senses; a sepulchre, grave

nésajjika-dhutanga (Sinhala, Sri Lanka) a religious observance which restrains a man from sleeping or lying down

an-avakānkshamāna (Sanskrit) not wishing impatiently (said of ascetics who, having renounced all food, expect death without impatience)

anupabbajjā (Pali, India) giving up worldly life in imitation of another

Magic numbers

Certain groupings have particular significance, particularly in Southern Asia.

3 tam-cuong (Vietnamese) the three fundamental bonds – prince and minister, father and son, husband and wife

4 tu-linh (Vietnamese) the four supernatural creatures – dragon, unicorn, tortoise, phoenix

5 bani khoms (Yemeni) practitioners of the five despised trades (barber, butcher, bloodletter, bath attendant and tanner)

6 luc-nghe (Vietnamese) the six arts – propriety, music, archery, charioteering, writing and mathematics

7 saptavidha-ratnaya (Sinhala, Sri Lanka) the seven gems or treasures of a Chakrawarti king – chariot wheel, wife, jewel, elephant, horse, son, prime minister

8 ashtāng (Hindi) prostration in salutation or adoration, so as to touch the ground with the eight principal parts of the body, i.e. with the knees, hands, feet, breasts, eyes, head, mouth and mind

9 nasāya-ratna (Sanskrit) the nine precious gems (pearl, ruby, topaz, diamond, emerald, lapis lazuli, coral, sapphire and garnet) which are supposed to be related to the nine planets

10 dasa-mūtraka (Sanskrit) the urine of ten (elephant, buffalo, camel, cow, goat, sheep, horse, donkey, man and woman)

Whistling in the wind

If your god isn't interested you may just have to fall back on other means:

itinatalagá (Tagalog, Philippines) to place oneself at the mercy of fate

uhranout (Czech) to cast the evil eye on somebody, to bewitch someone

bino (Gilbertese, Oceania) an incantation to get a woman back by turning a gourd very rapidly and allowing the wind to whistle into the opening

naffata (Arabic) a woman who spits on the knots (in exercising a form of Arabian witchcraft in which women tie knots in a cord and spit upon them with an imprecation)

The crystal ball

You might think that the advice of spirits and gods would be enough to comfort and direct humankind, but not a bit of it. We are so desperate to know what the future holds for us that almost anything will do:

fakane (Bugotu, Solomon Islands) to divine, using a broken coconut shell

koffiedik kijken (Dutch) reading tea leaves, predicting the future (literally, coffee-grounds-looking)

ber-dreymr (Old Icelandic) having clear dreams as to the future

lowa (Setswana, Botswana) a particular pattern in which a diviner's bones have fallen

onnevalamine (Estonian) telling one's fortune by pouring molten lead into cold water (on New Year's Eve)

chichiri-wiirik (Buli, Ghana) a man who can call on fairies to reveal things to him; a type of diviner

vayasa mutírtsu (Telugu, India) a crow crossing from the left side to the right (which Hindus consider a good omen)

Fringed with noodles

We all hope things will turn out well but there are all kinds of superstitions that wishing each other good luck might bring its reverse. When someone in Norway goes fishing, he is wished **skitt fiske**, lousy fishing.

German has two expressions for being lucky: **Schwein haben**, to have a pig – as a pig symbolizes good luck and lots of sausages; and **Sott haben**, to have soot – because, according to folklore, touching a chimney sweep brings luck. The French describe someone who is incredibly lucky as **il a le cul bordé de nouilles**, literally, his arse is fringed with noodles.

When pigs fly

na kukovo ljato (Bulgarian) in a cuckoo summer

kad na vrbi rodi grožđe (Croatian) when willows bear grapes

når der er to torsdage i en uge (Danish) when a week has two Thursdays

quand les poules auront des dents (French) when hens have teeth

am Sankt Nimmerleinstag (German) on St Never-ever-day

majd ha piros hó esik (Hungarian) when it's snowing red snowflakes

quando Pasqua viene a maggio (Italian) when Easter falls in May

tuyaning dumi yerga tekkanda (Uzbek) when the camel's tail reaches the ground

când o fi bunica fată mare (Romanian) when my grandma will be a virgin again

kag-da rak svist-nyet (Russian) when the crayfish whistles

balık ağaca / kavağa çıkınca (Turkish) when fish climb
   trees/poplar trees
cuando las ranas críen pelos (Spanish) when frogs grow
   hair